HOME BAKED *comfort*

RECIPES AND TEXT   KIM LAIDLAW

PHOTOGRAPHS   ERIC WOLFINGER

weldon**owen**

CONTENTS

WHY BAKE?

For as long as I can remember, I've been in the kitchen, covered in flour. I started baking before I could even read, my mom patiently instructing me how to cut butter into flour for flaky pie dough and biscuits or how to knead dough for a loaf of honey-wheat bread. The resulting treat was my motivation, whether it was a juicy and fragrant peach pie, tender biscuits topped with my grandmother's raspberry jam, or a thick slice of homemade bread slathered with butter.

Over the years I've grown downright passionate about baking, an activity that now feels natural and familiar to me. But I realize it's not like that for everyone. Some people find baking intimidating or daunting, but it needn't be so! In these pages, I hope to show that baking can be fun, relaxing, and achievable for everyone. It's also a wonderful way to bring folks together, to share in the process of baking as well as reap the delicious rewards.

The recipes gathered in this book are a mixture of family favorites and modern renditions on timeless classics, and also include a selection of treats from expert bakers and well-known bloggers across the country, each illustrating their personal style and approach to baking. Every one makes my mouth water. From puffy cinnamon rolls and spiced pumpkin coffeecake with brown sugar–pecan streusel to gooey s'mores brownies, mini lemon meringue tart bites, and decadent dulce de leche layer cake, there is something here to satisfy every sweet tooth. Savory items are plentiful as well: bacon-and-egg breakfast tarts; wild mushroom, chicken, and leek potpies; and billowy southern spoon bread with Cheddar cheese.

All in all, this book is about homemade goodness, made with lots of love. Each recipe is a little (or sometimes a lot) over-the-top. And while all the treats will surely fill your house with amazing aromas, the best part of baking is the process. From stirring the batter to pulling the finished cake out of the oven to taking the first bite of your sweet creation, baking brings friends and family together. So turn on your oven, get out your mixing bowl, and spread the joy of baking!

TEN TIPS
FOR BECOMING A BETTER BAKER
(AND ENJOYING IT)

1 PREPARE TO HAVE FUN

I can't stress this enough, and that's why it's my #1 tip. The goal is to have fun with baking. If you already love to bake, you can skip to tip #2. But if you're a bit intimidated, take a deep breath, close your eyes and imagine that delicious triple-layer chocolate cake. Honestly, what is the worst thing that could happen? Okay, so maybe it's a little lopsided. So what? It's gooey, delicious, and chocolatey—and likely ten times better than anything you buy. And if it's not perfect, you can try again another time (see tip #8). The point is, the more you relax, the more you'll enjoy baking, and this will be reflected in your end results.

2 GET READY

Skim through the recipe. Do you have all the ingredients? Think about the timing in advance: some recipes might call for batters or finished baked goods to be chilled, occasionally overnight. Once you understand how the recipe works, gather the ingredients and equipment you'll need. Then, prep your pans and set them aside so they'll be ready when you are. Letting a cake batter sit while you are buttering and flouring the pans can mean the difference between a light, airy cake and a heavy, dense one.

3 PREHEAT YOUR OVEN

You don't want to start with a cold oven, so make sure to preheat it at least 15 minutes prior to baking. Oven heat is what makes cakes rise, pie crusts crisp and flaky, and custards thicken. You need it for each and every recipe in this book.

4 USE THE BEST-QUALITY INGREDIENTS

Fresh ingredients really do make a difference, and your baked goods will shine a lot brighter if you purchase best-quality essentials like sweet butter, unbleached flour, ripe seasonal fruits, newly harvested nuts, and high-end chocolate from a trusted source that has fairly high turnover (bulk bins are often a great option).

5 A LITTLE BIT OF SALT ENHANCES FLAVOR

It's important to add a bit of salt, even if just a pinch, to many baked goods and desserts, as it will enhance the sweetness and natural flavors. Throughout the book, you'll notice that I put salt in almost every baked treat that I make, whether it's sweet or savory. I prefer to use kosher salt, which is what is listed in the recipes, but many people also love sea salt, which is a good substitute. If you do use sea salt, use slightly less than what is called for in the recipe as sea salt often has a more fine grain than kosher salt.

6 GET YOUR HANDS DIRTY

Think back to when you were a kid and you liked to touch everything. (Remember making mud pies in the backyard?) Put your hands in the bowl, touch the dough, and get to know what it feels like. Your hands are often your best tool for smoothing out ingredients into an even layer, sensing if a dough is the right consistency, or knowing if your cake has finished baking.

7 DON'T OVERWORK YOUR PASTRY

Yeast dough is one thing, but pastry dough—such as pie dough and biscuit dough—doesn't need a lot of handling. My motto with pastry dough is that less is more. Making it in the food processor keeps your warm hands off of it, which is important. And a good rule of thumb is to stop processing it before you think you should. Leave those chunks of butter in there. You want to see streaks when you roll out the dough. All those streaks equal light, flaky layers. Also, be sure to keep your pastry cold, especially on a hot day. If it starts to get warm and soft, just pop it into the refrigerator for 10 minutes before you continue.

8 PRACTICE MAKES PERFECT

The more time you spend in the kitchen, the more comfortable you'll feel there. And the more time you spend baking, the more you'll understand how ingredients interact and what you can and can't get away with. More importantly, you'll start to perfect your techniques. Few people can whip up a perfectly fluffy meringue the first time. To become more adept at baking is to pick an item you really love, say, pie. Make it over and over. Try different recipes. See what you like best about each one, and then keep making it. It may take time, but I guarantee you'll become good at it.

9 BE WILLING TO EXPERIMENT, AND TO FAIL

If you aren't very confident about baking, by all means follow the recipe...the first, and maybe even the second, time. But then, don't be afraid to mess with the ingredients a little. Try a different fruit, or a combination of fruits, or throw in a shot of whisky. I find that the more I experiment, the more at home I feel in the kitchen. And if the recipe doesn't work out, try something different the next time. Just keep trying.

10 ENJOY THE END RESULT

Who doesn't love freshly baked anything? One of the main reasons I bake is to enjoy the results with my friends and family. Invite someone over for tea and ginger cookies. Bring a chocolate-raspberry cake to a birthday party. Make a cherry pie for a weekend picnic. Share your gifts from the oven, and you'll not only feel a sense of pride and accomplishment, but you'll make everyone around you extremely happy.

TOP BAKING TOOLS
I CANNOT LIVE WITHOUT

These are the baking tools I use most often in my own kitchen, and what you'll see time and time again in the recipes throughout this book. This is by no means an exhaustive list, but I find each and every one of these items to be essential.

THE OVEN

It's a good idea to get to know your oven. Every oven works a bit differently, whether it's new or vintage; gas, electric, or convection; high-end or a hand-me-down. They all have their quirks, and sometimes can have hot spots or run hotter or cooler than the temperature you are aiming for. If you can, get your oven calibrated. At the very least, buy an oven thermometer so you know what you are dealing with.

STAND MIXER OR ELECTRIC MIXER

I love my KitchenAid stand mixer. It's durable and versatile, and I know it will be around for many years to come. It does great work kneading yeast doughs, making crumbly pastry doughs, and beating eggs and butter. Make sure you have the essential attachments for your mixer: whisk, paddle, and dough hook. Stand mixers are bulky and can be expensive, so the next best thing is a good-quality, sturdy handheld electric mixer. Although the hand mixer won't knead dough, it is invaluable for beating egg whites, creaming butter, and general mixing purposes.

BENCH SCRAPER AND PLASTIC SCRAPER

You might not be familiar with these two gems, but I use them constantly when I'm baking. A bench scraper has a rectangular stainless-steel blade, which makes quick work of dividing dough into portions or scraping dough off a work surface. A pastry scraper, a thin rectangle made of flexible plastic, allows you to easily scrape batter or dough from a bowl or off your rolling pin. Magic!

HEATPROOF RUBBER OR SILICONE SPATULA

I use a flexible spatula for countless tasks, whether folding whipped egg whites into a batter, stirring a warm custard on the stove top, or scraping cake batter into a baking pan. I recommend buying a heatproof version, especially after having melted a few myself. It's a good idea to have two sizes, a small spatula and a medium one, for different jobs.

GOOD-QUALITY PARING KNIFE

A top-notch paring knife makes peeling and slicing a breeze. Choose one with a 3- to 4½-inch (7.5- to 11.5-cm) forged blade and a comfortable handle. I suggest investing in a reputable brand—it will last longer and will ultimately earn its keep.

REALLY GREAT BREAD KNIFE

The serrated edge of a bread knife is ideal for slicing that warm, fresh bread you just baked (hence the name!). It also makes chopping blocks of chocolate and slicing through cake layers much, much easier than using a non-serrated blade. Look for a bread knife with at least a 10-inch (25-cm) forged blade and a sturdy handle.

ROLL OF PARCHMENT PAPER

Moisture- and grease-resistant parchment paper is a baker's secret weapon. I think it's the ideal thing for lining a baking sheet. You can also use it to line cake pans or to help roll out pie dough more easily. To do the latter, just put a disk of dough between 2 sheets of parchment and then roll out as directed; the paper prevents the dough from sticking to the work surface and the rolling pin.

MEASURING CUPS AND SPOONS

Have a set of measuring cups for dry ingredients and a glass measuring pitcher (with at least 1 cup/8 fl oz/250 ml capacity) for wet ingredients. Measuring cups for dry and wet ingredients aren't interchangeable, so be sure to use the appropriate vessels for each ingredient. Also, have a set of measuring spoons on hand; I like mine to be attached by a ring so I don't lose them.

SMALL DIGITAL SCALE

I use my digital scale for loads of things, from weighing flour, chocolate, and pieces of fruit to portioning out dough into equal pieces (you'll notice this in several recipes throughout the book). All you need is a small, flat scale that is decent quality, preferably showing both grams and ounces for use with a variety of recipes.

RIMMED BAKING SHEETS

Buy two heavy-duty, commercial-quality rimmed half-sheet baking pans (silver in color, not dark or nonstick). They will last for years even with heavy use, and they won't warp or buckle like cheap, thin, flimsy baking sheets I see in many kitchens. As a bonus, they will also help protect your yummy baked treats from burning on the bottom.

HEAVY-DUTY BAKING PANS AND DISHES

Quality, commercial-grade cake, bread, pie, tart, and muffin pans yield the best results and will last for years. Try to avoid aluminum pans, as they are often poor quality and cause uneven baking. Keep in mind that different materials are best for baking certain dishes. Having a few good-quality glass or ceramic dishes in standard sizes, such as a 9-inch (23-cm) square or 9-by-13-inch (23-by-33-cm) rectangle, is also useful.

AT LEAST THREE MIXING BOWLS

This one's easy: have on hand three nested bowls, small, medium, and large. Whether you choose stainless steel or ceramic is up to you, but you want bowls that are fairly heavy-duty and won't slide all over the place when you are beating egg whites or other mixtures. Nested bowls are nice simply because they take up less storage room and give you a range of sizes.

WIRE COOLING RACK

It's a really good idea to have one big wire cooling rack (mine is rectangular and about the size of a half-sheet baking pan). Make sure that it has little feet to raise it slightly off a surface so that air can flow underneath. I also like having a smaller rack on hand that I can use for inverting cakes.

BALLOON WHISK AND SMALL WHISK

Whisks are great not only for whipping up billows of cream or lighter-than-air meringue by hand but also for evenly mixing and aerating dry ingredients, stirring batters, keeping custard or melted chocolate smooth on the stove top, and more. A large balloon whisk is a staple. I also find that a smaller whisk is handy for beating together a few whole eggs or for small amounts of ingredients.

PASTRY BRUSH

The brush I use more than any other in my kitchen is a small silicone pastry brush, which is handy for washing down sugar crystals when making caramel, brushing egg wash or cream over biscuits or pie before baking, or glazing baked goods fresh out of the oven. It's easy to clean and heat resistant. You can also use a good-quality natural bristle brush.

SIFTER

I believe in sifting, and I love my rickety old vintage hand-crank sifter. Your best bet is a double- or triple-screened sifter, but you can also use a fine-mesh sieve. Whether or not it's called for in a recipe (and it is in many recipes in this book), sifting dry ingredients—flour, cocoa, baking soda—helps to aerate them, remove any lumps or clumps, and combine them. Sifting will ultimately make for light and airy baked goods.

ALL ABOUT INGREDIENTS

These are the building blocks of the decadent, mouthwatering recipes that you'll be baking throughout this book. Buy the best quality ingredients you can afford, and always try to find ripe fruit that's in season. If you start with the good stuff, you're on the right path to making truly delicious baked treats.

FLOUR

Flour is quite possibly the most important ingredient in the baker's pantry; it plays a vital role in the flavor, texture, and structure of baked goods. I generally use all-purpose flour in this book and strongly advise that you purchase a good-quality brand of organic unbleached all-purpose flour, as it has a cleaner, less chemical flavor than bleached flour.

Every so often a recipe will call for cake flour or whole-wheat flour. Just remember that cake flour and all-purpose flour are not interchangeable; cake flour has less protein and is more velvety in texture, perfect for certain cakes or biscuits with fine crumbs. Whole-wheat flour should be purchased fresh and stored in the refrigerator, as it will start to taste a bit funny if it gets old. For this book I use what's called white whole-wheat flour, which is lighter than regular whole-wheat flour.

BUTTER

I always use unsalted butter when I bake. The butter is fresher (salt is a preservative, which also means that salted butter is likely less fresh than unsalted by the time you purchase it), and I have more control over the amount of salt I add to the recipe. Make sure to use the freshest butter possible—in other words, don't use the stick of butter that's been sitting in the back of the refrigerator for three months. You can store butter in the freezer if you don't use it very often. Also, choose a good-quality butter. Some lesser-quality butters have a higher water content and minimal flavor, and you will notice a difference in your final product. If you need room-temperature butter, remove it from the refrigerator about half an hour before it is needed; it should be slightly cool to the touch, but pliable.

EGGS

The best eggs, of course, would be from your own chicken coop. But for most of us, it's best to get the freshest possible organic eggs. They come in a variety of sizes, but you'll need only large eggs for the recipes in this book. Always store eggs in the refrigerator, in the cardboard carton, away from foods with strong odors, which can be absorbed by the eggs during storage.

DAIRY

Buttermilk, whole milk, sour cream, and crème fraîche are used copiously throughout this book. Dairy products add fat to your baked treats, which contributes richness and tenderness. With the exception of buttermilk, which is commonly low-fat, skip fat-free or low-fat versions for the most flavorful and delicious results.

VANILLA

There's almost nothing that smells as amazing as vanilla, whether it's a fresh vanilla bean pod or a bottle of pure vanilla extract. When using a vanilla bean, make sure it's soft and pliable, which ensures freshness. To use, slice it lengthwise with a paring knife and use the back of the knife to scrape out the seeds. Always choose pure vanilla extract, not the chemical-tasting imitation version.

SALT

Whether savory or sweet, salt will help enhance the flavor of anything you bake. My hands-down personal preference is kosher salt. It has a more nubbly texture and "cleaner" flavor than regular, iodized salt, which can taste like chemicals to me. If you want to use a finer salt, such as fine sea salt, be sure to cut the amount called for in these recipes slightly, or it could be overkill.

SUGAR

From superfine to coarsely-grained and bright white to deep, dark brown, there are many different types of sugar. The most common sugar is granulated, liked for its subtle sweetness and ability to be transformed into golden caramel. Light and dark brown sugar add lots of flavor, and many of the recipes here call for light, with dark reserved for rich treats like gingerbread and butterscotch. Coarse sugar, such as turbinado or demerara, is ideal for sprinkling over the top of your baked goods for a finishing crunch.

NUTS AND COCONUT

The taste of toasted nuts and sweet, milky coconut add a wonderful dimension of flavor and texture to baked treats. From almonds to walnuts, buy the freshest nuts you can find, preferably from a market with a high turnover, and only buy what you need, as they can spoil quickly. Always sample nuts before you use them, and ideally store them in the refrigerator.

To toast nuts or shredded dried coconut, preheat the oven to 325°F (165°C). Spread the nuts or coconut in a single layer on a baking sheet and toast, stirring occasionally, until fragrant and lightly golden, 5–10 minutes for coconut, and 10–20 minutes for nuts.

CHOCOLATE

These days, we are lucky to be surrounded by an abundance of scrumptious chocolate. It truly does make a difference in the finished cake or pudding if you use a high-quality brand of chocolate or cocoa; no matter what you're making, buy the best you can find.

For bittersweet or semisweet chocolate, choose one that contains 60 to 75 percent cacao solids.

For milk chocolate, look for a "darker" version that's around 40 percent cacao. Keep in mind that European chocolates are usually less sweet and have a deeper, more refined flavor than American-made chocolates.

For cocoa powder, I use a natural, unsweetened, high-quality brand. The powder should be a rich, dark brown, not gray or light in color. I tend to avoid Dutch-process cocoa, which is milder in flavor.

CITRUS—PARTICULARLY LEMONS

You might guess this after looking at the recipes in this book: my all-time favorite ingredient is the lemon. Lemons brighten up everything and can be used in both sweet and savory recipes. A little zest adds zing and depth of flavor. A touch of lemon juice can help fruits shine (and stop them from turning brown before they are baked).

Whatever type of citrus is called for in a recipe, whether limes, oranges, or Meyer or Eureka lemons, look for heavy fruits that have shiny skins and aren't rock hard. For recipes calling for citrus zest, a Microplane zester is handy, as it takes off just the outer layer, leaving the bitter white pith behind. Before juicing a lemon (or a lime or an orange), roll it around on the work surface with the heel of your hand to help release the juice, then strain the extracted juice into a bowl before measuring to remove any seeds.

A side note about Meyer lemons: I adore Meyers. Their fragrant sweetness is like a cross between a tangerine and a lemon. You'll see them occasionally throughout the book. Unfortunately, they aren't readily available everywhere, so if you can't find them, substitute regular lemons.

FRUIT

I can't stress this enough: buy fruit in season. Just because you can find a peach in February in the supermarket doesn't mean it's a good peach. It's not worth it. Purchasing fruits in their natural growing season, when they are both plentiful and cheap, ensures that you will be rewarded with the sweetest, juiciest, most flavorful fruits.

Look for fruits that are free of bruises and blemishes, and feel heavy for their size. When you sniff them, they should have a full aroma.

Here's a quick guideline for finding the best fruits throughout the year:

Spring: rhubarb, strawberries

Summer: stone fruits (peaches, nectarines, cherries, apricots, plums, pluots); berries (blueberries, strawberries, blackberries, raspberries); figs

Fall/Winter: figs (early fall), citrus, apples, pears, grapes

AMAZING BAKING FACTS YOU MIGHT NOT KNOW

YOU CAN FREEZE DOUGH

Pie dough, cookie dough, dough for scones, and more—you can make the dough in advance and freeze it for a quick and easy from-scratch treat. For pie dough, prepare a double batch, divide it, and flatten each portion into a disk. Place the disks in a lock-top plastic freezer bag or wrap each disk in plastic wrap, and use them within a few months. (Freezing the dough can sometimes make pastry even flakier.) For cookies, biscuits, or scones, prepare the dough, portion it out onto a baking sheet, and put the baking sheet in the freezer. Transfer the individual frozen portions into a lock-top plastic freezer bag and use as much or as little as you want at a time.

YOU CAN MAKE YEAST DOUGH THE DAY BEFORE

This is true for virtually any yeast dough recipe. Prepare the dough, knead it, and let it rise as described in the recipe. After the first rise, punch down the dough to release the gases, divide and shape it if required, then cover with plastic wrap and refrigerate overnight. This works particularly well for gooey cinnamon rolls (page 32). Pizza dough and bread dough will develop more flavor the longer you chill the dough.

EGGSHELLS ARE MAGNETIZED

Okay, that's not strictly true, but if tiny eggshell fragments fall into a bowl of egg whites or yolks, you can scoop them up with an emptied half shell, and they readily cling to it. They are almost drawn to it as if magnetized! This works far better than using your fingers, a spoon, or the tip of a knife.

YOU CAN WHIP FLUFFIER EGG WHITES IN COPPER

If you own an unlined copper bowl, use it to whip egg whites without adding cream of tartar, which helps stabilize them. The copper reacts chemically with the egg proteins to produce tall, fluffy, stable whites with a satiny finish.

YOU CAN WARM UP EGGS IN A FLASH

When your recipe calls for room-temperature eggs, you don't need to put everything on hold while you wait for them to warm up from the refrigerator. Put the eggs in a bowl of lukewarm water for 10 or 15 minutes, and they'll be ready. Warm egg whites whip up better than cold, but use cold eggs if you want to separate the yolks and whites—you'll have a much easier time.

SALT ENHANCES THE FLAVORS OF SWEET TREATS

It might sound a bit odd, but adding salt helps bring out the sweetness and flavor of baked goods, even if they are sweet! To see for yourself, do an experiment. Make two batches of something, leave out the salt in one, and do a taste test. I bet you'll like the salted version better.

A NOTE ON BAKING TIMES

Whenever my husband asks how long something takes to cook or bake, I always answer, "Until it's done." I'm not trying to be coy...it's the truth! Although you should follow the timing in each recipe as a guide, every oven is slightly different, and may run a bit too hot or a bit too cold, thus causing your recipe to take slightly shorter or longer than the suggested timing. A good practice is to check early and keep checking, but not too often or you'll let all the heat out of your oven. Don't be afraid to touch the baked item. Also, watch the color: if it becomes too dark and still isn't baked through, lay a piece of foil over the top to prevent overbrowning.

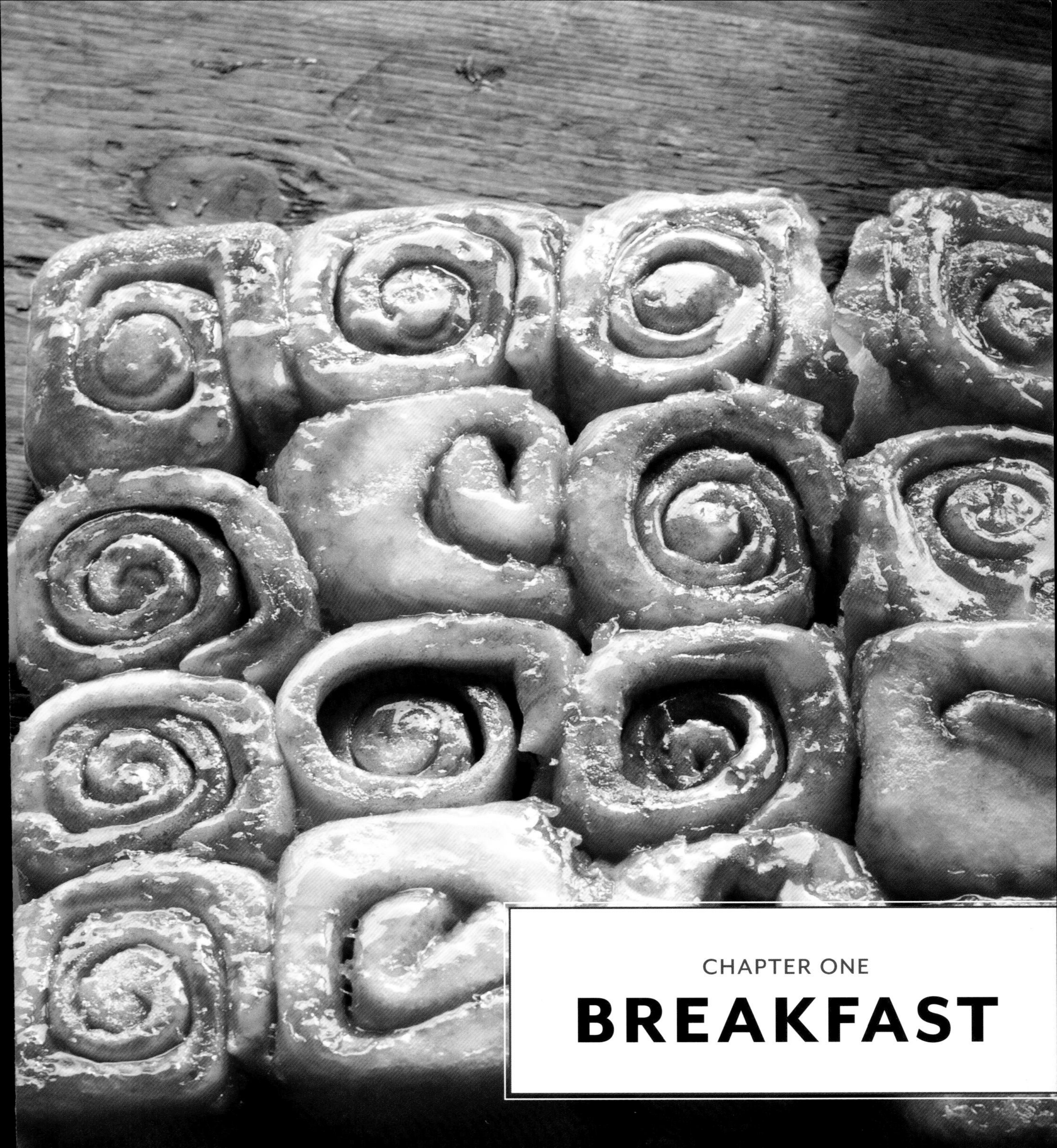

CHAPTER ONE

BREAKFAST

COFFEECAKE MUFFINS

With buttery streusel on top and a hidden layer of sticky jam, these muffins will make breakfast fun for everyone. I like to eat them with a big, steaming cup of joe while reading the Sunday newspaper.

for the streusel

¼ cup (1½ oz/45 g) all-purpose flour

¼ cup (2 oz/60 g) firmly packed light brown sugar

3 tbsp cold unsalted butter, cut into chunks

for the batter

2 cups (10 oz/315 g) all-purpose flour

2 tsp baking powder

½ tsp baking soda

¼ tsp kosher salt

½ cup (4 oz/125 g) cold unsalted butter, cut into chunks

½ cup (4 oz/125 g) granulated sugar

2 large eggs

2 tsp pure vanilla extract

1 cup (8 oz/250 g) sour cream

¼ cup (2½ oz/75 g) of your favorite preserves, such as peach, apricot, or blackberry

makes 12 muffins

Position a rack in the middle of the oven and preheat to 400°F (200°C). Line 12 standard muffin cups with paper liners, or grease with butter.

To make the streusel, in a bowl, stir together the flour and brown sugar. Scatter the butter over the top and work it in with your hands until the mixture forms small chunks. Put the streusel in the freezer while you make the batter.

To make the batter, in a bowl, sift together the flour, baking powder, baking soda, and salt. In the bowl of a mixer fitted with the paddle attachment, beat the butter and granulated sugar on medium-high speed until fluffy, about 1 minute. Beat in the eggs, one at a time, then the vanilla, until well combined, scraping down the sides of the bowl with a rubber spatula. Add the sour cream and beat on low speed to combine. Add the dry ingredients and, using the rubber spatula, stir just until evenly moistened. The batter will be quite thick.

Spoon a heaping tablespoon of the batter into each of the prepared muffin cups, enough to cover the bottom. Spoon a teaspoon of the preserves into the center of the batter in each cup. Top each with another spoonful of batter. The cups should be full. Sprinkle each with a big pinch of the streusel.

Bake until the muffins are golden brown and a toothpick inserted into the center of a muffin comes out clean, about 15 minutes. Let the muffins cool in the pan on a wire rack for about 5 minutes, then unmold onto the rack. Eat while they're still warm!

BAKER'S NOTE

Make sure you don't let the muffins sit in the pan too long to cool, as the bottoms will become soggy. Use a hot pad to tip the muffins out onto a cooling rack, gently prying those that are holding on tight. When all else fails, a paring knife can help coax any stubborn muffins from the pan.

MINI CHOCOLATE
CHIP–ALMOND MUFFINS

Decadent and sweet, these are the perfect party muffins. It's a little too easy to pop one (or two, or three!) into your mouth. This recipe makes quite a lot, so halve it if you want, but you'll probably be sorry you did.

1½ cups (7½ oz/235 g) all-purpose flour	2 large eggs
2 tsp baking powder	1 tsp pure vanilla extract
½ tsp baking soda	1 cup (8 fl oz/250 ml) buttermilk
¼ tsp kosher salt	1 cup (5 oz/150 g) mini chocolate chips
⅔ cup (3 oz/90 g) sliced almonds	
½ cup (4 oz/125 g) sugar	makes about 3 dozen mini muffins
½ cup (4 oz/125 g) cold unsalted butter, cut into chunks	

Position a rack in the middle of the oven and preheat to 400°F (200°C). Line two 24-cup mini-muffin pans with paper liners, or grease with butter.

In a bowl, sift together the flour, baking powder, baking soda, and salt. In a food processor, grind ½ cup (2 oz/60 g) of the almonds and the sugar to make a fine meal. Pour into the bowl of a stand mixer fitted with the paddle attachment and scatter the butter over the top. Beat on medium-high speed until fluffy, about 1 minute. Beat in the eggs, one at a time, then the vanilla, until well combined, scraping down the sides of the bowl with a rubber spatula. Add the buttermilk and beat on low speed. Add the dry ingredients and chocolate chips and, using the rubber spatula, stir just until evenly moistened.

Spoon the batter into the prepared muffin cups. Roughly chop the remaining almonds and sprinkle over the top. Bake until the muffins are golden brown and a toothpick inserted into the center of a muffin comes out clean, about 11 minutes, rotating the pans about halfway through. Let the muffins cool in the pans on a wire rack for about 5 minutes, then unmold onto the rack. Serve warm.

BAKER'S NOTE

Flavor these muffins by adding the zest of an orange to the batter—a stunning combination. Or, embellish the tops with coarse sugar, such as turbinado, just before you bake them.

ANGEL BISCUITS

Being a southern girl, I'm a bit obsessed with biscuits. I've made hundreds of renditions of baking powder biscuits and buttermilk biscuits in my quest to achieve the light-as-air disks I remember from my childhood. When I discovered angel biscuits, also known as "bride's biscuits," my search was over. Three forms of leavening means that they are guaranteed to rise into fluffy little pillows. Even though they take a bit of planning ahead, they are definitely worth it.

1 package (2¼ tsp) active dry yeast

1 tsp sugar plus a pinch

¼ cup (2 fl oz/60 ml) warm water (about 110°F/43°C)

3 cups (15 oz/470 g) soft-wheat flour, such as White Lily, or all-purpose flour

2 tsp baking powder

½ tsp baking soda

1 tsp kosher salt

6 tbsp (3 oz/90 g) frozen unsalted butter plus 2 tbsp melted butter

¼ cup (2 oz/60 g) very cold non-hydrogenated vegetable shortening, cut into small pieces

1 cup (8 fl oz/250 ml) plus 2 tbsp cold buttermilk

Honey Butter (page 215) or jam for serving

makes about 15 biscuits

In a small bowl, dissolve the yeast and pinch of sugar in the warm water. Let stand until foamy, about 10 minutes. Line a baking sheet with parchment paper.

In a large bowl, combine the flour, baking powder, baking soda, salt, and 1 teaspoon sugar and mix with your hands. Using the large holes of a grater-shredder, shred the 6 tablespoons butter into the bowl. Add the shortening and mix with your hands. You should see crumbly chunks of butter and shortening. Pour in the buttermilk and yeast mixture and mix just until the dry ingredients are moistened and start to come together. Be careful not to overmix the dough.

Dump the dough onto a lightly floured work surface and press into a disk about ¾ inch (2 cm) thick. Use a 2¾-inch (7-cm) biscuit cutter to stamp out as many biscuits as you can. Gather the scraps, roll out again, and cut out more biscuits.

Arrange the biscuits on the prepared baking sheet, cover loosely with plastic wrap, and set aside until puffed, about 1 hour, then refrigerate for a couple of hours or up to overnight. (You can also freeze the cut-out dough, tightly wrapped, for about 1 month.)

Position a rack in the upper third of the oven and preheat to 400°F (200°C). Brush the biscuits with the 2 tablespoons melted butter. Bake until the biscuits are golden brown, about 18 minutes. Remove from the pan and set on a wire rack to cool slightly. Serve warm with the honey butter or jam.

BAKER'S NOTE

For a real southern treat, serve these biscuits alongside freshly baked ham with a pot of good-quality mustard.

ORANGE-BERRY MUFFINS

Bursting with tart-sweet berries and flavored with a hint of orange zest, these tender muffins are an easy grab-and-go option for breakfast during the week. Loved by even the pickiest eaters, they make a welcome addition to any brunch menu.

2 cups (10 oz/315 g) all-purpose flour

2 tsp baking powder

½ tsp baking soda

¼ tsp kosher salt

½ cup (4 oz/125 g) cold unsalted butter, cut into chunks

⅔ cup (5 oz/155 g) granulated sugar

Finely grated zest from 1 orange

2 large eggs

1 tsp pure vanilla extract

1 cup (8 oz/250 g) sour cream

Heaping ½ cup (2 oz/60 g) fresh blueberries

Heaping ½ cup (2 oz/60 g) fresh raspberries

Coarse sugar, such as turbinado, for sprinkling (optional)

Butter for serving (optional)

makes 12 muffins

Position a rack in the middle of the oven and preheat to 400°F (200°C). Line 12 standard muffin cups with paper liners, or grease with butter.

In a bowl, sift together the flour, baking powder, baking soda, and salt. In the bowl of a mixer fitted with the paddle attachment, beat the butter, granulated sugar, and orange zest on medium-high speed until fluffy, about 1 minute. Beat in the eggs, one at a time, then the vanilla, until well combined, scraping down the sides of the bowl with a rubber spatula. Add the sour cream and beat on low speed. Add the dry ingredients and, using the rubber spatula, stir just until evenly moistened. Gently fold in the berries. The batter will be super thick.

Using a ¼-cup (2–fl oz/60-ml) measure (or an ice cream scoop), heap the batter into the prepared muffin cups, filling them nearly full. Sprinkle each with a big pinch of coarse sugar, if you like. Bake until the muffins are golden brown and a toothpick inserted into the center of one comes out clean, 15–17 minutes. Let the muffins cool in the pan on a wire rack for about 5 minutes, then unmold onto the rack. Smear them with butter if you like, and eat while they're still warm.

BAKER'S NOTE

This is a great basic muffin recipe that's fun to experiment with, depending on what fruit is in season or what's in your fridge. Two of my favorite flavor combinations are chopped fresh apricots with diced crystallized ginger and fresh pitted cherries with toasted almonds.

Flour Bakery + Cafe is Boston's answer to the sweet life. Step into one of its sunny locations for mouthwatering pastries and a friendly staff that takes pride in their decidedly warm service. You won't want to leave.

WHAT DO YOU LIKE MOST ABOUT OWNING A BAKERY?

I love making peoples' days happier. From our customers to our staff, Flour helps bring a little joy into peoples lives either with a delicious, sweet treat or by offering a great work environment for learning. That makes me really proud.

WHAT'S THE BEST PART OF YOUR DAY?

Visiting each location, saying hi to the staff, and eating everything I can!

WHAT MAKES YOUR BAKERY UNIQUE?

At Flour, we pride ourselves on every item passing the "mom test." If we wouldn't give it to our moms, we won't put it out for our customers.

WHAT'S YOUR FAVORITE COOKBOOK?

That's way too hard! Baking with Julia *was so inspiring to me when I was opening Flour. I also adore* Tartine. *I can't put down* Hot Sour Salty Sweet. The Cake Bible *has truly been a bible to me and Rose's [the author] voice is in my head when I bake.* Amy's Bread *is incredible. I just can't stop at one.*

PIE OR CAKE?

Wow, that's a tough question to answer! It depends on the kind. If it's a fruit pie, then pie. If it's a simple cake, then cake.

FLOUR
BROWN SUGAR–CRANBERRY OAT MUFFINS

Studded with tart cranberries and packed with wholesome oats, these delicious muffins bake up moist, with nicely rounded, golden-brown tops. A popular item at Flour Bakery + Cafe, customers enjoy them for breakfast with a tall glass of freshly squeezed orange juice.

1⅓ cups (7 oz/220 g) all-purpose flour

2 tsp baking powder

½ tsp baking soda

½ tsp kosher salt

2¼ cups (6½ oz/200 g) rolled oats

¾ cup (6 oz/185 g) crème fraîche

½ cup (4 fl oz/125 ml) whole milk, at room temperature

½ cup (4 oz/125 g) unsalted butter, melted and cooled

2 large eggs, lightly beaten

1 cup (7 oz/220 g) firmly packed brown sugar

1 cup (4 oz/125 g) chopped fresh or frozen cranberries

makes about 16 muffins

Position a rack in the middle of the oven and preheat to 350°F (180°C). Line 16 standard muffin cups with paper liners, or butter or oil the cups.

In a bowl, whisk together the flour, baking powder, baking soda, and salt. In another bowl, stir together 2 cups (6 oz/185 g) of the oats, the crème fraîche, milk, and butter until combined. Add the eggs, then the brown sugar, and stir until combined. Gently stir the dry ingredients into the oat mixture. Fold in the cranberries.

Fill the prepared muffin cups to the rims. Sprinkle the remaining ¼ cup (½ oz/15 g) oats evenly over the muffins. Pour a little water into any empty muffin cups to prevent scorching. Bake until the muffins are golden brown and a toothpick inserted into the center of a muffin comes out clean, about 25 minutes. Let the muffins cool in the pan on a wire rack for about 5 minutes, then unmold onto the rack to cool slightly. Serve warm.

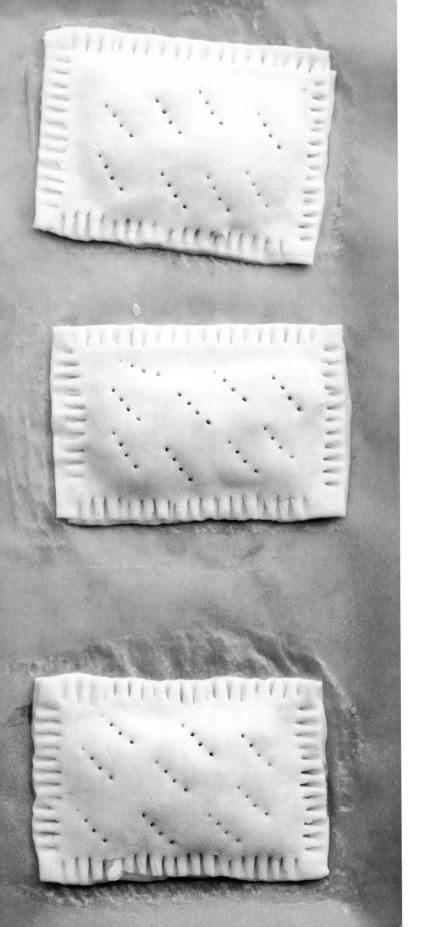

SOUR CHERRY "TOASTER" TARTS

I'm a child of the 1970s, and though my mom baked fresh bread, made her own yogurt, and had a vegetable garden, there was a certain amount of junk food that my brother and I always asked for. I loved cherry Pop-Tarts as a kid. I haven't had one in many years, so I thought I'd create a somewhat adult version of the pastry (but don't put these in the toaster!).

for the dough

2 cups (10 oz/315 g) all-purpose flour

¼ cup (1 oz/30 g) confectioners' sugar

½ tsp kosher salt

10 tbsp (5 oz/155 g) unsalted butter, cut into chunks

1 large egg yolk

⅓ cup (3 fl oz/80 ml) plus 2 tbsp whole milk

for the filling

¾ cup (7½ oz/235 g) sour cherry jam, or your favorite flavor

2 tsp cornstarch mixed with 1 tsp cold water

1 large egg beaten with 1 tsp warm water

for the glaze

1 cup (4 oz/125 g) confectioners' sugar, sifted

2 tsp whole milk

2 tsp corn syrup

½ tsp pure vanilla extract

Sprinkles (optional)

makes 12 toaster tarts

BAKER'S NOTE

You can embellish the tarts with all sorts of fancy sprinkles, or stir a little food coloring into a portion of the glaze and sling it across the top. Experiment with your favorite types of jam to re-create a Pop-Tart flavor you loved as a kid.

To make the dough, in a food processor, combine the flour, confectioners' sugar, and salt and process until blended. Add the butter and process until the mixture looks like coarse crumbs. Add the egg yolk and milk and process until the dough just comes together. Dump the dough onto 2 large sheets of overlapping plastic wrap. Press the dough into a disk, wrap with the plastic wrap, and refrigerate for about 30 minutes or overnight.

To make the filling, in a small saucepan, cook the jam and cornstarch mixture over medium heat, stirring, until slightly thickened and bubbly. Let cool.

Line 2 baking sheets with parchment paper. On a lightly floured work surface, divide the dough in half and form each half into a rough rectangle. Roll one rectangle until it measures about 16 by 9 inches (40 by 23 cm). Using a ruler and a pizza cutter, cut the dough into 12 small rectangles, each about 3 by 4 inches (7.5 by 10 cm). Set the rectangles on a baking sheet and refrigerate while you repeat with the other piece of dough.

Lay half of the rectangles on the work surface and lightly brush with the beaten egg. Dollop a tablespoon of the filling into the center of each. Spread it out on the dough, leaving a border of about ½ inch (12 mm). Top with a plain dough rectangle and press the edges together with your fingertips, being careful not to let the filling ooze out the sides. Crimp the edges with a fork. Put 6 tarts on each baking sheet, spacing them evenly, and prick the centers all over with the fork. Refrigerate while the oven preheats.

Position 2 oven racks evenly in the oven and preheat to 375°F (190°C). Bake the tarts, rotating the pans once halfway through, until golden brown, 15–18 minutes. Let cool on a wire rack.

Meanwhile, to make the glaze, whisk together the confectioners' sugar, milk, corn syrup, and vanilla until smooth. Smear the glaze on the tarts and decorate with sprinkles, if you like.

GOOEY CINNAMON ROLLS

for the dough

1 package (2¼ tsp)
active dry yeast

¾ cup (6 fl oz/180 ml)
whole milk, warmed
(110°F/43°C)

¼ cup (4 oz/125 g)
granulated sugar

4 large eggs

4½ cups (22½ oz/
705 g) all-purpose flour,
plus more as needed

1½ tsp kosher salt

6 tbsp (3 oz/90 g)
unsalted butter, at
room temperature,
cut into chunks

for the filling

4 tbsp (2 oz/60 g)
unsalted butter, at
room temperature,
cut into chunks

⅔ cup (5 oz/155 g)
firmly packed light
brown sugar

2 tsp ground cinnamon

Finely grated zest
of 1 large orange

1 egg, lightly beaten
with 1 tsp water

Cream Cheese Frosting
(page 214)

makes 16 buns

To make the dough, in the bowl of a stand mixer, dissolve the yeast in the warm milk and let stand until foamy, about 10 minutes. Add the granulated sugar, eggs, 4½ cups flour, and salt. Attach the dough hook and knead on low speed, adding a little more flour if needed, until the ingredients come together. Toss in the butter and continue to knead until the dough is smooth and springy, about 7 minutes. Lightly oil a large bowl. Form the dough into a ball, put it in the oiled bowl, and cover the bowl with plastic wrap. Let the dough rise at room temperature until it doubles, 1½–2 hours.

Butter a 9-by-13-inch (23-by-33-cm) baking dish. Punch down the dough and turn out onto a lightly floured work surface. Cut it in half.

Roll out 1 dough half into a rectangle about 9 by 14 inches (23 by 35 cm). Spread with half of the butter, then sprinkle evenly with half of the brown sugar, half of the cinnamon, and half of the grated zest. Starting at the long side closest to you, roll the rectangle away

from you, forming a log. Cut the log crosswise into 8 equal slices. Arrange the slices, cut side down, in half of the prepared pan. Repeat with the remaining dough and filling ingredients, and arrange the slices in the other half of the pan. Cover the pan loosely with plastic wrap and let stand in a warm, draft-free spot until puffy, about 1 hour, or refrigerate overnight, then let stand at room temperature for 30–60 minutes before baking.

Position a rack in the middle of the oven and preheat to 400°F (200°C). Brush the buns lightly with the beaten egg. Bake until the rolls are golden brown and a toothpick inserted into the center of a roll comes out clean, 20–25 minutes. Let the rolls cool slightly in the pan on a wire rack, then spread with the frosting while they are still warm. Pull the rolls apart and enjoy while they're warm.

Honestly, there is quite possibly no better aroma than a pan of these big, puffy rolls baking in the oven, fragrant with cinnamon, brown sugar, and orange zest.

BAKER'S NOTE

If you like, add ⅓ cup (2 oz/60 g) raisins or toasted chopped pecans to the filling. If you prepare these the night before up until the final rise and baking, then all you have to do in the morning is let them come to room temperature and then slide them in the oven to bake.

CARAMEL-PECAN
STICKY BUNS

Ooey, gooey, sticky, messy, gorgeous, and decadent pecan sticky buns: If you, like me, have a sweet tooth as big as Texas, these are the perfect medicine. Make them when you want to impress your guests, or win someone's heart.

for the dough

1 package (2¼ tsp) active dry yeast

¾ cup (6 fl oz/180 ml) whole milk, warmed (110°F/43°C)

¼ cup (2 oz/60 g) granulated sugar

4 large eggs

4½ cups (22½ oz/ 705 g) all-purpose flour, plus more as needed

1½ tsp kosher salt

6 tbsp (3 oz/90 g) unsalted butter, at room temperature, cut into chunks

for the caramel

6 tbsp (3 oz/90 g) butter, melted

1 cup (7 oz/220 g) firmly packed light brown sugar

3 tbsp dark honey

Pinch of kosher salt

1 cup (4 oz/125 g) coarsely chopped pecans

for the filling

4 tbsp (2 oz/60 g) butter, at room temperature

½ cup (3½ oz/105 g) firmly packed light brown sugar

1 tsp ground cinnamon

makes 16–20 buns

BAKER'S NOTE

For something a little out of the ordinary, try replacing the pecans in these buns with roughly chopped almonds. Throw in a handful of dried cherries to boot.

To make the dough, in the bowl of a stand mixer, dissolve the yeast in the warm milk and let stand until foamy, about 10 minutes. Add the granulated sugar, eggs, 4½ cups flour, and salt. Attach the dough hook and knead on low speed, adding a little more flour if needed, until the ingredients come together. Toss in the butter and continue to knead until the dough is smooth and springy, about 7 minutes. Lightly oil a large bowl. Form the dough into a ball, put it in the oiled bowl, and cover the bowl with plastic wrap. Let the dough rise at room temperature until it doubles, 1½–2 hours.

Butter two 9-inch (23-cm) round cake pans.

To make the caramel, stir together the melted butter, brown sugar, honey, salt, and pecans. Spread half of the pecan mixture in each pan.

Punch down the dough and dump onto a floured work surface. Cut it in half. Roll out each half into a rectangle about 8 by 14 inches (20 by 35 cm). Position the rectangles horizontally.

To fill the rolls, spread each rectangle with 2 tablespoons of the butter, then half of the brown sugar and half of the cinnamon, leaving ½ inch (12 mm) of the side closest to you uncovered. Starting at the side farthest from you, roll up the rectangle into a log. Pinch the seams to seal. Cut each log crosswise into 8 or 10 equal slices. Arrange the slices, cut side up, in each pan. Cover the pans loosely with plastic wrap and let stand in a warm, draft-free spot until puffy, about 1 hour, or refrigerate overnight, then let stand at room temperature for 30–60 minutes before baking.

Position a rack in the middle of the oven and preheat to 350°F (180°C). Bake until the buns are golden brown, 30–35 minutes. Let cool in the pans on a wire rack for 5 minutes, then carefully invert each pan onto a plate and unmold the buns. When they are still warm, but cool enough not to burn your fingers, pull them apart and dig in.

LEMON CREAM SCONES

I am partial to British-style scones—I'm always on the hunt for the perfect recipe—which are more tender and biscuitlike than the often dense and crumbly American pastries. This version is one of my favorites, and it appeases my wistful cravings for the real deal on the other side of the pond.

3 tbsp granulated sugar

Grated zest and juice of 2 lemons

2 cups (10 oz/315 g) all-purpose flour

2 tsp baking powder

¼ tsp kosher salt

½ cup (4 oz/125 g) cold unsalted butter, cut into small chunks

¾ cup (6 fl oz/180 ml) heavy cream, plus extra for brushing

¼ cup (1 oz/30 g) confectioners' sugar, sifted

Raspberry Jam (page 214) or your favorite jam, for serving (optional)

makes 8 scones

Position a rack in the middle of the oven and preheat to 400°F (200°C). Line a baking sheet with parchment paper.

In the bowl of a mixer, stir together the granulated sugar and lemon zest. Sift the flour, baking powder, and salt into the bowl and stir together. Scatter the butter over the top. Using the paddle attachment, mix on low speed until the butter is about the size of small peas, about 3 minutes.

Strain the lemon juice into a small bowl and measure out ¼ cup (2 fl oz/60 ml), reserving the rest. Add the ¼ cup lemon juice and ¾ cup cream to the bowl and mix just until the dough comes together. The dough will be thick but moist.

Dump the dough onto a floured work surface and gently press into a disk about ¾ inch (2 cm) thick. Cut into 8 equal wedges (or cut into circles using a 2-inch/5-cm biscuit cutter). Place the wedges on the prepared baking sheet, spacing them apart. Brush with cream. Bake until the scones are golden brown, 15–17 minutes. Remove from the pan and set on a wire rack to cool slightly.

While the scones are cooling, in a small bowl, stir together the confectioners' sugar and 2 teaspoons of the reserved lemon juice. Brush or drizzle the glaze over the scones. Serve warm with jam, if desired.

BAKER'S NOTE

You can easily turn these into classic cream scones with currants by omitting the lemon zest and lemon juice from the dough and the glaze at the end. Stir in ¼ cup (2 oz/60 g) dried currants once you've added the cream. You might need a touch more cream if the dough is too dry. Cut the dough into rounds with a biscuit cutter, and serve the scones with clotted cream (if you can find it) and jam.

BAKERELLA
MINI BANANA-MAPLE PANCAKE MUFFINS

These gems are like little banana pancakes baked into muffin shapes, which makes them easy to pop into your mouth. For the sweetest flavor, use an overly ripe banana; and to take these over the top, toss ½ cup (3 oz/90 g) mini chocolate chips into the batter.

1 cup (5 oz/155 g) all-purpose flour

2 tbsp sugar

1 tsp baking powder

½ tsp baking soda

¼ tsp kosher salt

⅔ cup (5 fl oz/160 ml) buttermilk

1 large egg

2 tbsp pure maple syrup, plus more for dipping

2 tbsp unsalted butter, melted

1 very ripe, large banana, mashed

makes 2 dozen mini muffins

Position a rack in the middle of the oven and preheat to 350°F (180°C). Generously grease 24 mini muffin cups with nonstick cooking spray or grease with butter.

In a large bowl, whisk together the flour, sugar, baking powder, baking soda, and salt. In another bowl, stir together the buttermilk, egg, 2 tablespoons maple syrup, and the butter until just combined. Add the wet ingredients to the dry ingredients and stir until combined. Stir in the mashed banana.

Spoon the batter into the prepared muffin cups. Bake until the muffins are puffed and golden, 10–12 minutes. Let the muffins cool slightly in the pan on a wire rack, then unmold onto the rack. Serve right away with maple syrup for dipping.

ANGIE DUDLEY
WWW.BAKERELLA.COM

Angie Dudley, a baking enthusiast, is the mastermind behind not only these tasty miniatures, but many more easy-to-follow recipes on her popular blog, Bakerella. You'll find oodles of sweet baking fun, decorating tips, and treats ranging from cheesecake and pies to brownies and cookies. But her specialty is cake pops—little bites of cake and frosting, dipped in candy coating and put on a stick—which are the delicious phenomenon behind her award-winning website.

PUMPKIN COFFEECAKE
WITH BROWN SUGAR–PECAN STREUSEL

This is, hands down, my favorite coffeecake recipe. Lighter than you would expect, with the rich flavor of pumpkin and spices, and a thick layer of crunchy brown sugar and pecan streusel, it would make an ideal dish for the winter holidays or for a festive autumn brunch.

for the streusel

⅓ cup (2 oz/60 g) all-purpose flour

½ cup (3½ oz/105 g) firmly packed light brown sugar

1 tsp ground cinnamon

Pinch of kosher salt

6 tbsp (3 oz/90 g) cold unsalted butter, cut into small chunks

1 cup (4 oz/125 g) chopped pecans, lightly toasted (see note)

for the batter

1½ cups (7½ oz/235 g) all-purpose flour

2 tsp baking powder

½ tsp baking soda

2 tsp ground cinnamon

1 tsp ground ginger

¼ tsp freshly grated nutmeg

½ tsp kosher salt

½ cup (4 oz/125 g) unsalted butter

1 cup (7 oz/220 g) firmly packed light brown sugar

2 large eggs

½ cup (4 oz/125 g) pumpkin puree

½ cup (4 oz/125 g) sour cream

for the glaze

½ cup (2 oz/60 g) confectioners' sugar, sifted

1 tsp whole milk

1 tsp pure vanilla extract

makes one 9-inch (23-cm) coffeecake

Position a rack in the middle of the oven and preheat to 350°F (180°C). Butter and flour a 9-inch (23-cm) springform pan or a 9-inch cake pan with 3-inch (7.5-cm) sides.

To make the streusel, in a bowl, combine the flour, brown sugar, cinnamon, and salt. Toss in the butter and, using 2 table knives or a pastry cutter, cut it into the dry ingredients until the mixture looks like coarse crumbs. (Or you can whir the mixture in a food processor as I do.) Stir in the pecans.

To make the batter, in a bowl, sift together the flour, baking powder, baking soda, cinnamon, ginger, nutmeg, and salt. In the bowl of a mixer fitted with the paddle attachment, beat the butter and brown sugar on medium-high speed until well combined. Beat in the eggs, one at a time, scraping down the sides of the bowl with a rubber spatula. Add the pumpkin puree and sour cream and mix with the spatula. Stir in the flour mixture. The batter will be quite thick. Spread half of the batter in the prepared pan. Sprinkle half of the streusel over the batter. Dollop the remaining batter over the streusel and spread the thick batter as best you can. Top with the remaining streusel. Bake until a toothpick inserted into the center of the cake comes out clean, about 50 minutes. Let cool in the pan on a wire rack for about 15 minutes. Remove the sides from the pan and slide the cake onto the rack.

To make the glaze, in a small bowl, whisk together the confectioners' sugar, milk, and vanilla. Drizzle over the top of the cake. Cut into thick wedges and serve with big steaming cups of joe.

BAKER'S NOTE

To toast pecans, preheat the oven to 325°F (160°C). Spread the nuts out on a rimmed baking sheet and bake, stirring often, until fragrant and lightly toasted, about 10 minutes.

BROWN BUTTER DUTCH BABY
WITH CARAMELIZED PEARS

This breakfast dish can easily be dessert—and, in fact, it probably should be. But however you serve it, this oven-baked pancake is light, eggy perfection. Often made with apples, the classic is known by many names, such as German pancake, oven pancake, and, my favorite, Dutch baby.

4 large eggs, lightly beaten

⅔ cup (5 fl oz/160 ml) whole milk

⅔ cup (3 oz/90 g) all-purpose flour

1 tbsp granulated sugar

1 tsp pure vanilla extract

½ tsp kosher salt

4 tbsp (2 oz/60 g) unsalted butter

for the caramelized pears

1 tbsp unsalted butter

3 tbsp firmly packed light brown sugar

3 ripe pears, such as Bosc or Anjou, peeled, cored, and sliced

Juice of ½ lemon

Confectioners' sugar for dusting

makes 6 servings

Position a rack in the lower third of the oven and preheat to 425°F (220°C).

In a blender, blend together the eggs, milk, flour, sugar, vanilla, and salt. In a 10-inch (25-cm) cast-iron pan, melt 3 tablespoons of the butter over medium heat, swirling it in the pan. Let it bubble, swirling occasionally, until it starts to turn nutty brown. Add the browned butter to the batter and blend to mix. Put the remaining 1 tablespoon butter in the pan and place in the oven to melt the butter. Swirl the butter around the pan, then pour the batter into the pan and bake for 15 minutes without opening the oven door. Reduce the oven temperature to 375°F (190°C) and bake until puffed and golden, about 10 minutes.

While the Dutch baby is baking, cook the pears: In another frying pan, melt the butter over medium-high heat. Add the brown sugar, pears, and lemon juice and cook, stirring, until the pears are tender and sticky, about 8 minutes.

Spoon the pears into the center of the Dutch baby, dust with confectioners' sugar, and serve right away.

BAKER'S NOTE

Turn this modern version back into a classic by swapping out the pears for apples and adding a sprinkle of cinnamon. Or, personalize it by using whatever peeled and sliced fruit you have on hand, such as bananas, peaches, or apricots.

CHRISTMAS
BREAKFAST PIE

Every Christmas morning, for as long as I can remember, I woke up to the smell of this cinnamony breakfast pie baking in the oven. Before we were allowed to open presents, everyone helped themselves to a warm slice. Regardless of whether we are together, my mom, my brother, and I still carry on the tradition to this day.

for the dough

1 package (2¼ tsp) active dry yeast

½ cup (4 oz/125 g) granulated sugar plus 1 tbsp

1 cup (8 fl oz/250 ml) warm water (about 110°F/43°C)

3 cups (15 oz/470 g) all-purpose flour

½ tsp kosher salt

1 large egg

4 tbsp (2 oz/60 g) unsalted butter, melted

3 tbsp light olive oil

for the filling

2 cups (1 lb/500 g) whole-milk ricotta cheese

2 large egg yolks

½ cup (4 oz/125 g) granulated sugar

2 tbsp all-purpose flour

½ tsp ground cinnamon

Finely grated zest of 1 orange

Juice of ½ lemon

for the streusel

⅔ cup (4 oz/125 g) all-purpose flour

⅓ cup (3 oz/90 g) granulated sugar

⅓ cup (2½ oz/75 g) firmly packed brown sugar

1 tsp ground cinnamon

½ cup (4 oz/125 g) cold unsalted butter, cut into chunks

makes two 9-inch (23-cm) pies

To make the dough, in the bowl of a stand mixer, dissolve the yeast and 1 tablespoon granulated sugar in the warm water and let stand until foamy, about 10 minutes. Add the ½ cup granulated sugar, the flour, salt, egg, melted butter, and oil. Attach the paddle attachment and beat until well combined. The dough will be very sticky. Cover the bowl with plastic wrap and let rise in a warm place for about 1 hour.

Position a rack in the middle of the oven and preheat to 375°F (190°C). Generously butter two 9-inch (23-cm) pie pans.

To make the filling, in a bowl, stir together the ricotta, egg yolks, granulated sugar, flour, cinnamon, orange zest, and lemon juice.

To make the streusel, in another bowl, mix together the flour, granulated and brown sugars, and cinnamon. Toss in the butter and, using 2 table knives or a pastry cutter, cut it into the flour mixture until the mixture looks like chunky crumbs.

Using wet hands, divide the dough between the prepared pans. It will be very sticky. Do your best to press it evenly into each pan and up the sides to create a bowl shape (don't be afraid to show it who's boss!). Divide the filling between the dough-lined pans, then top each with half of the streusel. Bake until bubbly and golden brown, 30–40 minutes. Let cool for at least 15 minutes before serving.

BAKER'S NOTE

The dough in this recipe is very sticky. One way to deal with sticky dough is to make sure your hands are nice and wet before trying to maneuver it. If it starts to stick, simply rinse your hands again.

BITE-SIZE
BACON AND CHEESE SCONES

*I dare you to stop eating these!
Seriously, when I make these scones,
someone (usually my husband) has
to take them away from me. These
buttery, bacony, cheesy delights are
heaven in one easy bite. Perfect for brunch,
they would also make for a great lunch
alongside a bountiful salad.*

3 thick slices
applewood-smoked
bacon

2 cups (10 oz/315 g)
all-purpose flour

2 tsp baking powder

1 cup (4 oz/125 g)
grated Asiago or
Gruyère cheese

Pinch of kosher salt

½ tsp freshly
ground pepper

½ cup (4 oz/125 g)
cold unsalted butter,
cut into chunks

1 large egg

¾ cup (6 fl oz/180 ml)
heavy cream or
whole milk

makes about 4 dozen
mini scones

Position a rack in the middle of the oven and preheat to 400°F (200°C). Line a rimmed baking sheet with parchment paper.

In a frying pan, fry the bacon over medium-low heat until lightly crisp, about 5 minutes. Transfer to a cutting board and finely chop the bacon.

In a food processor, combine the flour, baking powder, cheese, salt, and pepper and pulse briefly to mix. Add the butter and pulse until the mixture looks like coarse meal. In a small bowl, whisk together the egg and cream until blended. Pour the egg mixture into the processor and pulse just until the dough comes together.

Dump the dough onto a lightly floured work surface. Knead in the bacon and then bring the dough together into a ball. Using a floured rolling pin, roll out the dough to ½ inch (12 mm) thick. Using a 1½-inch (4-cm) biscuit cutter, cut out as many scones as you can. Gather the scraps of dough, roll out, and cut out more scones.

Space the scones evenly on the prepared baking sheet. Bake until the scones are golden, about 12 minutes. Remove from the pan and let cool slightly on a wire rack before serving.

BAKER'S NOTE

To take these scones over the top, add a pinch
of grated cheese to the top of each one before
you slide them into the oven.

HAM, LEEK, AND GRUYÈRE QUICHE

Quiche is one of the most versatile dishes you can make. It can be varied with the seasons; accommodate a spectrum of cheeses, vegetables, and meats; and be served for breakfast, lunch, or dinner. This is one of my all-time favorite quiche combinations.

Flaky Pie Dough for single crust (page 212)

1 small leek, white and pale green parts

1 tbsp unsalted butter

Kosher salt and freshly ground pepper

1 thick slice Black Forest ham, about 6 oz (185 g), diced

2 large eggs

½ cup (4 fl oz/125 ml) whole milk

½ cup (4 oz/125 g) crème fraîche or sour cream

Heaping ½ cup (2 oz/60 g) shredded Gruyère cheese

makes one 9-inch (23-cm) quiche

BAKER'S NOTE

To give this quiche a special flourish, buy an extra leek, preferably a small one. Thinly slice the white and pale green parts lengthwise, and sauté them in butter until wilted. Lay the long leek slices on top of the quiche before you sprinkle it with cheese and bake.

Prepare the pie dough and chill as directed. On a lightly floured work surface, roll out the dough into an 11-inch (28-cm) round about ⅛ inch (3 mm) thick. Drape the dough over the rolling pin and ease it to a 9-inch (23-cm) tart pan with at least 1-inch (2.5-cm) sides and a removable bottom. Press the dough into the bottom and up the sides of the pan, then fold the edge over on itself and press together. Put the pan in the freezer and chill for about 15 minutes. Position a rack in the middle of the oven and preheat to 400°F (200°C).

Prick the bottom of the pie shell with a fork, then line with foil. Fill with pie weights or dried beans. Bake until the crust is set but not browned, about 12 minutes. Remove the foil and weights. Prick any bubbles with a fork. Continue to bake until the crust is firm and very lightly golden, about 5 minutes. Set the pan on a wire rack. Position the rack in the upper third of the oven and reduce the temperature to 375°F (190°C).

While the crust is baking, quarter the leek lengthwise and slice; you should have about 1 cup (4 oz/125 g). In a frying pan, melt the butter over medium heat. Add the leek and a pinch of salt, and cook, stirring occasionally, until the leek starts to brown and becomes tender, about 3 minutes. Toss the diced ham into the pan, stir to combine with the leek, and remove from the heat.

In a bowl, whisk together the eggs, milk, crème fraîche, a pinch of salt, and a few grinds of pepper. Scatter the ham and leeks evenly over the crust, pour in the egg mixture, and sprinkle the cheese on top. Place the pan on a rimmed baking sheet and bake until the quiche is puffed and lightly golden and a knife inserted into the center comes out clean, 25–30 minutes. If you like, slide the quiche under the broiler for a few minutes to brown the top a bit more. Let the quiche stand on the wire rack for about 10 minutes. Serve warm or at room temperature.

CHEESY HERB POPOVERS

These truly magnificent popovers puff and billow over the sides of the muffin pan during baking. It's best to eat them hot, fresh out of the oven, but be careful of the steam inside as you rip them apart.

3 large eggs
½ cup (4 fl oz/125 ml) heavy cream
1 cup (8 fl oz/250 ml) whole milk
1¼ cups (6½ oz/200 g) all-purpose flour
Scant tsp minced fresh thyme, chives, or oregano
¼–½ tsp kosher salt (depending on how salty the cheese is)

3 tbsp unsalted butter, melted
½ cup (2 oz/60 g) shredded Gruyère, Cheddar, or Parmesan cheese

makes 12 popovers

Position a rack in the middle of the oven and preheat to 425°F (220°C). Generously butter 12 standard muffin cups, including the top of the pan.

In a blender, process the eggs, cream, milk, flour, herbs, and salt until blended. With the blender running, pour in the melted butter. Pour the batter into the prepared muffin cups, filling them about three-fourths full. Top each with a sprinkle of cheese. Bake for 20 minutes (you may want to peek at the popovers, but whatever you do, don't be tempted to open the oven door).

Reduce the oven temperature to 350°F (180°C) and bake until the popovers are hollow and golden brown, about 15 minutes longer. Immediately unmold the popovers onto a wire rack. They are best eaten right away, while hot (but please don't burn yourself).

BAKER'S NOTE
Popovers can be either sweet or savory. If you are in the mood for sweet, omit the cheese and herbs to make plain popovers. Serve them with plenty of your favorite jam.

ZUCCHINI, BASIL, AND FONTINA QUICHELETS

These cute little quiches are perfect for a lunch alfresco. Serve them with bubbly prosecco, a fresh salad, and some sliced peaches and berries, and you have one gorgeous summer meal.

Flaky Pie Dough for single crust (page 212)

2 small zucchini, about 7 oz (220 g) total, trimmed

Kosher salt and freshly ground pepper

3 large eggs

½ cup (4 fl oz/125 ml) heavy cream or half-and-half

Scant tbsp finely chopped fresh basil

½ cup (2 oz/60 g) shredded fontina cheese

makes 4 quichelets

BAKER'S NOTE

You can easily turn this recipe into a regular-sized quiche by lining a 9-inch (23-cm) tart pan with the dough and partially baking as directed in the recipe. Add the entire amount of filling to the partially baked crust and bake as directed, although it might take a few more minutes to finish baking.

Prepare the pie dough and chill as directed. Position a rack in the middle of the oven and preheat to 400°F (200°C). Have ready four 4½-inch (11.5-cm) tartlet pans with removable bottoms.

Divide the dough into 4 equal pieces (I find that a kitchen scale works great for a job like this). On a floured work surface, roll each piece into a round about 6 inches (15 cm) in diameter. Line the pans with the rounds of dough. As you finish each one, put it in the freezer so it stays cold. Line each tart shell with foil and then fill with pie weights or dried beans. Put the shells on a baking sheet and bake until set and starting to dry out, about 15 minutes. Remove the foil and weights and continue to bake until the crusts look dry, about 5 minutes more. Remove from the oven. Reduce the oven temperature to 375°F (190°C).

While the crusts are baking, shred the zucchini on the large holes of a grater-shredder onto paper towels. Spread out the shreds and sprinkle with a little salt. Let sit for about 20 minutes. Using paper towels, blot the zucchini dry (try to get it as dry as possible). Divide the shredded zucchini among the tartlet shells. In a bowl, whisk together the eggs, cream, and basil. Season with salt and pepper. Divide the mixture among the pans, pouring it over the zucchini. Sprinkle with the cheese.

Bake until the filling is set and the tops are golden brown, about 25 minutes. If you want to get the cheese extra bubbly and brown, slide the quichelets under the broiler for 1 minute. Let sit for a few minutes before serving.

BACON-AND-EGG
BREAKFAST TARTS

When I was testing this recipe, I had the idea to crack an egg on top of each tart and then bake them together. The results were a bit of a disaster, to say the least. In the end, I fried the eggs separately and placed them on top of the baked tarts, which is easy and very pretty, too. Make these for a special brunch, especially if you want to impress your friends or in-laws.

1 sheet purchased frozen puff pastry, about 10 by 14 inches (25 by 35 cm), thawed

¾ cup (3 oz/90 g) shredded white Cheddar or Gruyère cheese

⅓ cup (2½ oz/75 g) crème fraîche or sour cream

12 thick slices applewood-smoked bacon

1 tbsp olive oil

6 large eggs

Kosher salt and freshly ground pepper

1 tbsp roughly chopped fresh chives

makes 6 tarts

BAKER'S NOTE

Use the best-quality puff pastry you can find. A local bakery will often sell fresh puff pastry, so check around. I also like Dufour brand, which is available in high-end markets. The same goes for eggs: the fresher your eggs, the more scrumptious your over-easy eggs will be.

Position a rack in the middle of the oven and preheat to 400°F (200°C). Line a baking sheet with parchment paper.

On a lightly floured work surface, roll out the pastry into a rectangle about 12 by 15 inches (30 by 38 cm). Trim the edges (I like to use a pizza wheel and a ruler to cut puff pastry). Cut the rectangle into 6 equal rectangles, each about 5 by 6 inches (13 by 15 cm). Using a small, sharp knife, cut a line around each rectangle about ½ inch (12 mm) from the edge. Do not to cut all the way through; you just want to create a ridge when the pastry is baked. Using a fork, prick the pastry inside the line all over. Lay the rectangles on the prepared baking sheet. Refrigerate while you prepare the toppings.

In a small bowl, stir together the shredded cheese and crème fraîche. In a large frying pan (it is best to choose a nonstick pan with a lid, so you only have to clean one pan), fry the bacon over medium-low heat until just barely crisped, about 5 minutes. Drain on paper towels. Discard the fat in the pan.

Dollop a spoonful of the cheese mixture in the center of each pastry rectangle and spread it out to the cut line. Roughly chop the bacon and sprinkle it over the cheese mixture. Bake until the pastry is puffed, crisp, and golden, about 15 minutes.

While the pastry is baking, fry the eggs: In the large frying pan, warm the olive oil over medium-low heat. Crack the eggs into the pan. Sprinkle with salt and a few grinds of pepper. Cover the pan (this is a handy trick for making beautiful over-easy eggs) and cook until the whites are cooked through and the yolks are still a bit runny.

Place the tarts on warmed plates and top each with a fried egg. Sprinkle with chives and serve.

CHAPTER TWO

BREADS

DARK AND STICKY GINGERBREAD

I really like gingerbread, but not nearly as much as my husband, who lights up like a kid at Christmastime whenever I make this dark, spicy, and ultramoist cake. It's perfect for a wintry day, and even better when paired with a frothy pint of Guinness.

1 cup (8 fl oz/250 ml) brewed espresso or very strong coffee

¾ cup (6 oz/185 g) firmly packed dark brown sugar

1 cup (11 oz/345 g) molasses (not blackstrap)

¾ cup (6 fl oz/180 ml) canola oil

3 large eggs, lightly beaten

2 tbsp peeled and grated fresh ginger

2 cups (10 oz/315 g) all-purpose flour

2 tsp baking powder

½ tsp baking soda

2 tbsp ground ginger

1 tsp ground cinnamon

¼ tsp freshly grated nutmeg

Pinch of ground white pepper

½ tsp kosher salt

Heaping ¼ cup (1½ oz/45 g) chopped crystallized ginger

Whipped Cream (page 214), for serving

makes one 9-inch (23-cm) gingerbread

Position a rack in the middle of the oven and preheat to 350°F (180°C). Butter the bottom and sides of a 9-inch (23-cm) springform pan. Line the bottom with parchment paper and butter the parchment. Put the pan on a rimmed baking sheet.

In a bowl, whisk together the espresso, brown sugar, molasses, oil, eggs, and fresh ginger. In a large bowl, sift together the flour, baking powder, baking soda, ground ginger, cinnamon, nutmeg, pepper, and salt. Add the wet ingredients along with the crystallized ginger, and stir to combine. The batter will be quite loose.

Pour the batter into the prepared pan and bake until a toothpick inserted into the center comes out clean, 50–60 minutes. Let cool for about 10 minutes, then remove the pan sides and slide the gingerbread onto a serving plate. Serve warm with heaps of whipped cream.

BAKER'S NOTE

Make the gingerbread into a dessert fit for company by serving slices topped with poached pears (use the recipe from the Winter Trifle, page 138) and cream whipped with a big pinch of ground ginger.

PUMPKIN-BRANDY BREAD

Growing up, I remember my mom baking this bread in metal coffee cans and how I loved the funny round shape. This recipe calls for a lot of brandy, more than you might be comfortable with, but it is honestly the best pumpkin bread I have ever tasted. You can cut the brandy in half if you want.

4 large eggs

2 cups (1 lb/500 g) granulated sugar

1 cup (7 oz/220 g) firmly packed light brown sugar

1 cup (8 fl oz/250 ml) canola oil

⅔ cup (5 fl oz/160 ml) brandy

1 can (15 oz/470 g) pumpkin puree

3½ cups (17½ oz/545 g) all-purpose flour

2 tsp baking soda

1½ tbsp pumpkin pie spice

1 tsp kosher salt

½ cup (2 oz/60 g) chopped pecans or walnuts, lightly toasted (page 15; optional)

makes 2 loaves

Position a rack in the middle of the oven and preheat to 350°F (180°C). Generously butter two 9-by-5-inch (23-by-13-cm) loaf pans.

In a large bowl, whisk together the eggs and sugars. Add the oil, brandy, and pumpkin and whisk to combine. In another bowl, sift together the flour, baking soda, pumpkin pie spice, and salt. Add to the pumpkin mixture along with the nuts, if using, and stir to combine.

Divide the batter between the prepared pans and bake until richly golden brown and a toothpick inserted into the center of a loaf comes out clean, about 50 minutes. Let cool slightly in the pans, then turn the loaves out onto a wire rack to cool.

BAKER'S NOTE

Baked in smaller, individual-sized loaf pans, this decadent bread makes excellent mini gifts during the holidays. Divide the batter between the pans. The baking time might vary depending on the size of the pans. Once the baked loaves have cooled, wrap each one in colorful cellophane, tie a ribbon around it, and bring on the good cheer.

SUPER BANANA BREAD

Warning: This bread is highly addictive. I don't call it "super" for nothing. Not only that, but I can't think of a better way to use those slightly-too-old bananas sitting in your fruit basket.

2 cups (10 oz/315 g) all-purpose flour

2 tsp baking powder

½ tsp baking soda

½ tsp kosher salt

½ tsp ground cinnamon

⅛ tsp freshly grated nutmeg

3 very ripe, large bananas, smashed

2 large eggs

1 cup (7 oz/220 g) firmly packed dark brown sugar

½ cup (4 oz/125 g) sour cream

1 tsp pure vanilla extract

4 tbsp (2 oz/60 g) unsalted butter, melted

Turbinado sugar for sprinkling

makes 2 loaves

Position a rack in the middle of the oven and preheat to 350°F (180°C). Generously butter two 9-by-5-inch (23-by-13-cm) loaf pans.

In a bowl, sift together the flour, baking powder, baking soda, salt, cinnamon, and nutmeg. In a large bowl, whisk together the bananas, eggs, brown sugar, sour cream, vanilla, and butter. Add the dry ingredients and stir to combine.

Divide the batter between the prepared pans and sprinkle with turbinado sugar. Bake until a toothpick inserted into the center of a loaf comes out clean, about 35 minutes. Let cool slightly in the pans, then turn the loaves out onto a wire rack to cool.

BAKER'S NOTE

To turn the bread into scrumptious banana-nut muffins, make the batter as directed, adding about ½ cup (2 oz/60 g) lightly toasted chopped walnuts or pecans. Line a 12-cup muffin pan with liners and fill with the batter. Bake for about 20 minutes or until a toothpick inserted into a muffin comes out clean.

LEMON-BLUEBERRY DRIZZLE BREAD

This extra lemony bread has a triple dose of lemon flavor: zest in the batter, syrup that you brush on while the bread is still warm, and a sweet lemon glaze drizzled over the top. I like to eat a slice in the middle of the afternoon with a steaming cup of tea.

1½ cups (7½ oz/235 g) all-purpose flour, plus 1 tsp

1 tsp baking powder

½ tsp kosher salt

½ cup (4 oz/125 g) unsalted butter, at room temperature

¾ cup (6 oz/185 g) granulated sugar

1 tbsp finely grated lemon zest

3 large eggs

½ cup (4 fl oz/125 ml) whole milk

1 tsp pure vanilla extract

1 cup (4 oz/125 g) fresh blueberries

for the syrup

3 tbsp fresh lemon juice

3 tbsp granulated sugar

for the glaze

½ cup (2 oz/60 g) confectioners' sugar

3 tsp fresh lemon juice

makes 1 large loaf

Position a rack in the middle of the oven and preheat to 350°F (180°C). Butter and flour a 9-by-5-inch (23-by-13-cm) loaf pan.

In a bowl, sift together the 1½ cups flour, baking powder, and salt. Set aside. In the bowl of a mixer fitted with the paddle attachment, beat the butter, granulated sugar, and lemon zest on medium-high speed until lightened. Add the eggs one at a time, beating until each is incorporated. Add the milk and vanilla and stir until blended. Add the dry ingredients and stir just until blended. In a small bowl, toss the blueberries with the 1 teaspoon flour. Gently stir into the batter.

Scrape the batter into the prepared pan. Bake until lightly browned and a toothpick inserted into the center comes out clean, about 50 minutes. Transfer the bread to a wire rack set over a rimmed baking sheet and let cool in the pan for a few minutes, then turn out onto the rack.

While the bread is baking, make the syrup: In a small saucepan, boil the lemon juice and granulated sugar over medium heat until syrupy, about 2 minutes. Remove from the heat. Using a wooden skewer, pierce the sides and bottom of the bread all over. Brush the bread generously with the syrup.

To make the glaze, in a small bowl, stir together the confectioners' sugar and lemon juice. When the bread is completely cool, drizzle the glaze over the top.

BAKER'S NOTE

In the wintertime, when blueberries aren't in season, make lemon-poppy seed bread. Omit the blueberries, and add a tablespoon of poppy seeds to the batter. Bake as directed.

HUCKLEBERRY

SANTA MONICA, CALIFORNIA

Huckleberry Café & Bakery is owned by husband-and-wife team Josh and Zoe, whose dream of a casual bakery where friends, family, and food lovers come together to eat mouthwatering baked goods and savory meals has come true. Zoe gave me a bit of background on the family-run bakery.

HOW WOULD YOU DESCRIBE YOUR BAKERY?

Abundant, fun, too loud, happy, joyful, tasty, love.

WHAT ARE TWO THINGS PEOPLE DON'T KNOW ABOUT YOUR BAKERY?

The idea for our bakery started out with my father and I hijacking our other restaurant, Rustic Canyon, on Saturdays and turning it into an impromptu bakery. To our surprise, it was a hit. So, we decided to open up an actual bakery down the street! Also that in our kitchen, contrary to popular belief, we don't believe that baking is an exact science.

WHAT'S THE BEST THING YOU BAKE?

Gosh, I don't know. I love corn bread, so I guess it would be our Blueberry Cornmeal Cake. I love having it with a scoop of vanilla ice cream.

WHAT'S FOR DINNER TONIGHT?

Honestly, I just put my three-and-a-half-month-old to bed and my husband and I had a peaceful hot meal of scrambled eggs and toast, sautéed asparagus, and a large glass of red wine. It was perfect.

IS THERE ANYTHING ELSE YOU WANT US TO KNOW ABOUT YOUR BAKERY?

It's a labor of love, but the main reason I do it is because I get to work alongside my husband and see my family everyday. And I get to be in a kitchen full of people I love!

Pumpkin Teacake
Slice $3.50 | Whole $30

Cinnamon Roll
$3.75 / each

Ginger
Teacake
$3.50

Donut Hole
$0.50

Wheat
ice
each

Huckleberry

HUCKLEBERRY
HOMEMADE ENGLISH MUFFINS

Flavored with the rich tang of buttermilk, these thick-cut English muffins are tender and slightly chewy, and nothing like what you buy at the grocery store. They are delicious straight out of the oven or toasted the next day, with plenty of butter and jam.

2 cups (16 fl oz/500 ml) buttermilk

3¾ cups (1 lb 5 oz/ 620 g) bread flour, plus more as needed

2 packages (4½ tsp) instant dry yeast

2 tbsp sugar

1½ tbsp kosher salt

2 tbsp honey

1 tbsp unsalted butter, at room temperature

Cornmeal for dusting

Butter and jam, such as Raspberry Jam (page 214), for serving

makes about 8 muffins

In a saucepan, warm the buttermilk over low heat to 120°F (49°C). Set aside.

In the bowl of a stand mixer fitted with the dough hook, combine the bread flour, yeast, sugar, and salt and mix together on low speed. Add the buttermilk in a steady stream, then add the honey and butter. Mix on low speed until the dough is almost smooth but still a little shaggy, about 3 minutes. Add a little more flour if the dough is very sticky.

Form the dough into a ball, place it back in the mixing bowl, cover with plastic wrap, and let rise in the refrigerator for at least 2 hours and up to 24 hours.

Line a rimmed baking sheet with parchment paper. Place the dough onto a work surface generously dusted with cornmeal and roll it out to about ¾ inch (2 cm) thick. Using a 3-inch (7.5-cm) biscuit cutter (or a glass or empty can), cut the dough into rounds (you'll have to knead the scraps together and re-roll the dough to cut the last few). Transfer the dough rounds to the prepared baking sheet. Cover loosely with plastic wrap and let rise until puffy, about 45 minutes.

Position a rack in the middle of the oven and preheat to 350°F (190°C). In a large dry skillet or griddle, preferably cast-iron, over medium heat, brown both sides of half the dough rounds, then quickly return them to the baking sheet. Repeat with the remaining dough rounds. Bake until puffed and golden brown, about 15 minutes. Let cool slightly, then split and serve with plenty of butter and jam.

HAZELNUT STREUSEL BREAD

This bread is a hazelnut lover's dream: a tender, nutty texture studded with melty chocolate chips and a thick layer of crunchy hazelnut streusel on top.

for the streusel

3 tbsp all-purpose flour

¼ cup (2 oz/60 g) firmly packed light brown sugar

1 tsp ground cinnamon

3 tbsp cold unsalted butter

½ cup (2½ oz/75 g) hazelnuts, toasted, peeled (see Note), and roughly chopped

for the batter

⅓ cup (2 oz/60 g) hazelnuts, toasted and peeled (see Note)

⅔ cup (5 oz/155 g) granulated sugar

1¼ cups (6½ oz/200 g) all-purpose flour

2 tsp baking powder

½ tsp baking soda

Scant ½ tsp kosher salt

6 tbsp (3 oz/90 g) unsalted butter, softened

2 large eggs

1 tsp pure vanilla extract

¾ cup (6 oz/185 g) sour cream or plain yogurt

½ cup (3 oz/90 g) miniature semisweet chocolate chips or chunks (optional)

makes 1 large loaf

To make the streusel, in a food processor, combine the flour, brown sugar, cinnamon, and butter and process until crumbly. Transfer to a bowl and stir in the ½ cup chopped hazelnuts. Set aside.

Position a rack in the middle of the oven and preheat to 350°F (180°C). Generously butter a 9-by-5-inch (23-by-13-cm) loaf pan.

To make the batter, in the food processor, process the ⅓ cup whole hazelnuts and half of the granulated sugar until finely ground. Add the flour, baking powder, baking soda, and salt. Process to combine and transfer to a large bowl.

In the food processor, process the butter and remaining granulated sugar until light and creamy, scraping down the sides of the bowl with a rubber spatula as you go. Add the eggs and vanilla and process until fully combined. Add the sour cream and process until combined. Scrape into the bowl with the dry ingredients and stir together. Stir in the chocolate chips, if using.

Scrape about half of the batter into the prepared pan. Sprinkle with about half of the reserved streusel. Dollop the rest of the batter over the streusel and spread it evenly in the pan, then top with the remaining streusel.

Bake until a toothpick inserted in the center of the loaf comes out clean, about 50 minutes. Let cool in the pan for about 10 minutes, then remove from the pan and let cool completely on a wire rack. Cut into slices to serve.

BAKER'S NOTE

If you can find them, purchase already peeled hazelnuts. Otherwise, spread them on a baking sheet and toast in a 325°F (165°C) oven for about 10 minutes, shaking the pan occasionally. Then, pour the warm nuts into a kitchen towel and rub them together to remove the skins. Don't worry about removing all the skins—the bread will still taste great.

BLACKBERRY
CORNMEAL SHORTCAKES

One of my all-time favorite desserts has to be strawberry shortcake. I remember hauling out the Bisquick baking mix as a kid and making shortcakes, then piling the warm cakes high with far too many summer strawberries and mounds of whipped cream. Here's a slightly more adult version of the same thing.

1¾ cups (9 oz/280 g) all-purpose flour

¼ cup (1½ oz/45 g) fine cornmeal

2 tsp baking powder

½ tsp baking soda

½ tsp kosher salt

1 tbsp sugar plus ¼ cup (2 oz/60 g)

1 cup (8 fl oz/250 ml) buttermilk

½ cup (4 oz/125 g) unsalted butter, melted and cooled

4 cups (1 lb/500 g) blackberries, halved if large

1 tbsp Chambord (optional)

Whipped Cream (page 214) for serving

makes 6 shortcakes

Position a rack in the middle of the oven and preheat to 400°F (200°C). Line a baking sheet with parchment paper.

In a bowl, whisk together the flour, cornmeal, baking powder, baking soda, salt, and 1 tablespoon sugar until blended. Add the buttermilk and butter and toss gently with a fork or rubber spatula until the flour is just moistened and the ingredients are blended.

Drop 6 equal-sized dollops of the batter onto the prepared pan, spacing them well apart. Bake until the shortcakes are puffed and golden, 15–18 minutes. Transfer to a wire rack to cool slightly.

While the shortcakes are baking, in a bowl, toss together the blackberries, ¼ cup sugar, and Chambord, if using, crushing a few of the berries. Cover and refrigerate until well chilled or until serving.

Split the shortcakes in half horizontally. Place the bottom halves on plates and spoon on some of the blackberries and juices. Top with big dollops of whipped cream, then the tops of the shortcakes, and dig in.

BAKER'S NOTE

If (like me) you can't resist strawberry shortcake, you can easily turn these into the classic version. Omit the cornmeal and use 2 cups (10 oz/315 g) flour for the biscuits. Instead of blackberries, substitute the same amount of sliced strawberries tossed with Grand Marnier.

KITCHEN SINK CORN BREAD

Since I'm from Texas, one of my favorite comfort foods is a big bowl of real Texas chili and a hunk of corn bread, which I use to dip liberally into the saucy meat. I don't have space here to share my chili recipe, so use your favorite one, but make sure to serve a pan of this golden bread alongside it.

1 cup (5 oz/155 g) fine cornmeal

1 cup (5 oz/155 g) all-purpose flour

2 tsp baking powder

½ tsp baking soda

½ tsp kosher salt

1 cup (6 oz/185 g) corn kernels, preferably fresh

2 large eggs

¼ cup (3 oz/90 g) honey

1⅓ cups (11 fl oz/ 330 ml) buttermilk

4 tbsp (2 oz/60 g) unsalted butter, melted

½ cup (2 oz/60 g) shredded sharp white Cheddar cheese

1 can (4 oz/125 g) chopped green chiles, drained and rinsed

1 jarred small roasted red bell pepper, finely chopped (about ¼ cup/ 2 oz/60 g)

Butter for serving

makes one 10-inch (25-cm) corn bread

Position a rack in the middle of the oven and preheat to 425°F (220°C). Generously butter a 10-inch (25-cm) cast-iron frying pan or square baking pan.

In a bowl, whisk together the cornmeal, flour, baking powder, baking soda, salt, and corn kernels.

In a large bowl, whisk together the eggs until blended. Add the honey, buttermilk, and butter and whisk until blended. Stir in the dry ingredients until evenly moistened. Add the cheese, chiles, and roasted pepper, and stir until just combined.

Scrape the batter into the prepared pan and smooth the top. Bake until a toothpick inserted into the center comes out clean, 20–25 minutes. Let the bread cool slightly in the pan on a wire rack. Serve warm with lots of butter.

BAKER'S NOTE

Make this recipe your own by adding or omitting ingredients. Want a hotter, simpler version? Add a couple of minced jalapeños instead of the roasted peppers and green chiles. Or add cooked, crumbled bacon, pepper Jack cheese, and sautéed onions instead of the Cheddar, chiles, and bell peppers.

BEER ROLLS

I remember making these with my brother when we were quite young. It was the easiest recipe—just Bisquick and beer—and we thought it was great when the batter would foam up as we added the beer. Plus we got to eat beer! This is my updated version of the rolls. I still love making them.

2 cups (10 oz/315 g) all-purpose flour	1 cup (8 fl oz/250 ml) lager-style beer
2 tsp baking powder	½ cup (4 oz/125 g) unsalted butter, melted and cooled
1 tsp sugar	
½ tsp baking soda	
½ tsp kosher salt	makes 12 rolls

Position a rack in the middle of the oven and preheat to 400°F (200°C). Line a baking sheet with parchment paper.

In a large bowl, whisk together the flour, baking powder, sugar, baking soda, and salt until blended. Add the beer and melted butter and gently toss with a fork or rubber spatula until the flour is just moistened and the ingredients are blended.

Drop 12 equal-sized dollops of the batter onto the prepared pan, spacing them well apart. Bake until the rolls are puffed and golden, 15–18 minutes. Transfer to a wire rack to cool slightly before serving.

BAKER'S NOTE

To turn the rolls into regular drop biscuits, substitute 1 cup (8 fl oz/250 ml) buttermilk for the beer and proceed with the recipe as directed.

FIGGY CARDAMOM BREAD

1 cup (8 fl oz/250 ml) whole milk, warmed (110°F/43°C)

1 package (2¼ tsp) active dry yeast

⅓ cup (3 oz/90 g) sugar, plus more for sprinkling

3½ cups (17½ oz/ 545 g) all-purpose flour

1 tsp kosher salt

1 tsp ground cardamom

3 large eggs

6 tbsp (3 oz/90 g) unsalted butter, at room temperature, cut into chunks

1½ cups (9 oz/280 g) quartered dried figs

makes 1 large loaf

In the bowl of a stand mixer, stir together the milk, yeast, and ⅓ cup sugar. Let stand until foamy, about 10 minutes.

In another bowl, whisk together the flour, salt, and cardamom. Add the dry ingredients and 2 of the eggs to the yeast mixture. Attach the dough hook and knead the dough on medium-low speed until it starts to look shaggy. While continuing to knead, add the butter. Knead until the dough is fairly smooth, about 10 minutes. Dump the dough onto a floured work surface and flatten into a disk. Scatter the figs over the dough and gather it into a ball. Knead the dough gently to incorporate the figs. Gather the dough into a ball, transfer to an oiled bowl, cover with plastic wrap, and let rise in a warm, draft-free spot until doubled, about 1 hour.

Line a baking sheet with parchment paper. Dump the dough onto the lightly floured work surface and divide it into 3 equal pieces. Roll each piece into a rope about 16 inches (40 cm) long.

Lay the ropes next to each other, touching, on the work surface. Braid the ropes together, tucking the ends underneath the braid. Place on the prepared pan, cover loosely with a kitchen towel, and let rise until puffy, about 45 minutes.

Position a rack in the middle of the oven and preheat to 350°F (180°C). In a small bowl, beat the remaining egg with a little water. Brush the dough gently with the egg wash, then sprinkle generously with sugar. Bake until golden brown, about 35 minutes. Let cool completely on a wire rack before slicing.

This braided loaf makes a stunning presentation and is easier to make than you might think. It's based on the traditional cardamom-spiked breads from Sweden and Finland, with luscious dried figs added for some sparkle.

BAKER'S NOTE

For a more traditional cardamom bread, omit the figs and top the bread with sliced almonds or toasted walnuts just before baking, then drizzle with vanilla glaze (page 214) after the bread cools for a bit. You can also top it with coarse sugar before baking.

CHOCOLATE-CHERRY
BUTTERMILK BUNS

I use a lot of buttermilk in my baked goods. The flavor is incomparable, and the consistency helps give baked goods (or waffles or pancakes) a luscious texture, both rich and moist. These qualities are especially noticeable in these buns, which are best eaten while still warm, when the chocolate is gooey.

1 package (2¼ tsp) active dry yeast

½ cup (4 oz/125 g) sugar

1¼ cup (10 fl oz/310 ml) buttermilk, warmed (110°F/43°C)

3 large eggs

3¼ cups (16½ oz/515 g) all-purpose flour

1½ tsp kosher salt

6 tbsp (3 oz/90 g) unsalted butter, at room temperature, cut into chunks

1 cup (6 oz/185 g) small chocolate chunks or chips

½ cup (3 oz/90 g) chopped dried cherries

makes 16 buns

In the bowl of a stand mixer fitted with the paddle attachment, dissolve the yeast and sugar in the buttermilk and let stand until foamy, about 10 minutes. Add 2 of the eggs, the flour, and the salt and mix on low speed until combined. Add the butter and beat on medium-high speed until the butter is incorporated. Fit the mixer with the dough hook and knead the dough on low speed for about 5 minutes. The dough will be very sticky. Add the chocolate and cherries and knead just long enough to incorporate them into the dough. Scrape the dough into a ball, cover the bowl with plastic wrap, and let rise in a warm, draft-free spot until it doubles, about 1½ hours.

Line a baking sheet with parchment paper. Dump the dough onto a lightly floured work surface and punch down. Divide into 16 equal pieces and shape each into a ball. If some of the chocolate and cherry chunks fall out, stick them back into the dough. Place the balls on the prepared pan, spacing them evenly, and cover with a kitchen towel. Set aside to rise until puffed, about 1 hour.

Position a rack in the middle of the oven and preheat to 350°F (180°C). In a small bowl, beat the remaining egg with a little water. Brush the buns gently with the egg wash. Bake until golden brown, about 25 minutes. Let cool slightly on a rack. The buns are best served the day they are baked and even better when they're eaten warm.

BAKER'S NOTE

Many people don't seem to know this, but buttermilk doesn't actually contain any butter—it was traditionally the leftover liquid after you churned butter out of cream. In the United States, buttermilk is usually a cultured milk that is surprisingly low fat.

BUTTERY FLAKY ROLLS

These truly must be the ultimate dinner roll. Soft, buttery, yeasty, they are what yearn for alongside a bowl of beef stew in the wintertime, or a big fresh dinner salad in the summer. They taste very decadent and will impress anyone you make them for.

6 tbsp (3 oz/90 g) unsalted butter, plus 3 tbsp, melted and cooled	1 large egg, lightly beaten
	3 cups (15 oz/470 g) all-purpose flour
2 tsp dark honey	2 tbsp sugar
1 cup (8 fl oz/250 ml) whole milk	1 tsp kosher salt
1 package (2¼ tsp) active dry yeast	makes 18 rolls

BAKER'S NOTE

If you don't want pull-apart rolls, instead of using cake pans, space the dough rounds on two parchment-lined baking sheets and then let rise and bake as directed.

In a small saucepan, melt the 6 tablespoons butter with the honey over low heat. Stir in the milk and gently warm the mixture to about 110°F (43°C). Pour into the bowl of a stand mixer. Stir in the yeast and let stand until foamy, about 10 minutes.

Stir in the egg, flour, sugar, and salt. Attach the dough hook and knead the dough on medium speed for about 5 minutes. The dough will be very soft and sticky. Form the dough into a ball, cover the bowl with plastic wrap, and let rise in a warm, draft-free spot until doubled, about 1½ hours.

Generously butter two 9-inch (23-cm) round cake pans. Dump the dough onto a floured work surface. Divide the dough into 18 equal pieces, each about 1½ ounces (45 g). (This is when a scale comes in handy!) Roll each piece into a ball and place 9 balls in each prepared pan, spacing them evenly. Brush the dough balls generously with 2 tablespoons of the melted butter. Cover loosely with plastic wrap and let stand until puffy, about 1 hour.

Position a rack in the middle of the oven and preheat to 375°F (190°C). Bake until the rolls are golden, about 18 minutes. Brush with the remaining 1 tablespoon melted butter as soon as they come out of the oven. Serve warm.

HOT CROSS
BUN LOAF

When I worked as a baker, hot cross buns were one of my favorite, most-loved recipes to make. Come Easter, we would turn them out by the hundreds. Here's a riff on the classic in loaf form, which is delicious sliced, toasted, and slathered with butter.

4 tbsp (2 oz/60 g) unsalted butter

1 cup (8 fl oz/250 ml) whole milk

¼ cup (2 oz/60 g) granulated sugar

1 package (2¼ tsp) active dry yeast

4 cups (1¼ lb/625 g) all-purpose flour

¾ tsp ground cinnamon

⅛ tsp ground allspice

⅛ tsp freshly grated nutmeg

1 tsp kosher salt

2 large eggs, lightly beaten

1 cup (6 oz/185 g) dried currants

1 tbsp finely grated orange zest

for the filling

4 tbsp (2 oz/60 g) unsalted butter, softened

⅔ cup (5 oz/155 g) firmly packed light brown sugar

1 tbsp ground cinnamon

1 egg white, beaten with a little warm water

for the glaze (optional)

½ cup (2 oz/60 g) confectioners' sugar

1 tsp pure vanilla extract

1 tsp whole milk

makes 2 loaves

In a small saucepan, melt the butter over low heat. Stir in the milk and granulated sugar, and warm to 110°F (43°C). Pour into the bowl of a stand mixer and add the yeast. Let stand until foamy, about 10 minutes.

In another bowl, whisk together the flour, cinnamon, allspice, nutmeg, and salt. Add to the yeast mixture along with the eggs, currants, and orange zest. Attach the dough hook to the mixer and knead the dough on medium-low speed for about 10 minutes. Scrape the dough into a ball, cover the bowl with plastic wrap, and let rise in a warm, draft-free spot until doubled, about 1½ hours.

Meanwhile, make the filling: In a bowl, stir together the softened butter, brown sugar, and cinnamon.

Butter two 9-by-5-inch (23-by-13-cm) loaf pans. Dump the dough onto a floured work surface. Divide the dough in half. Roll each half into an 8½-inch (21.5-cm) square. Smear each square with half of the filling. Roll up the dough, pinch the seam to seal, and place seam side down in a prepared pan. Let rise until puffy and the dough rises above the pan sides, 1–1½ hours.

Position a rack in the middle of the oven and preheat to 350°F (180°C). Brush the loaves with the egg wash. Bake until the loaves are golden brown and pull away from the pan sides, about 35 minutes. Turn out onto racks and let cool completely.

To make the glaze, if you like, in a small bowl, stir together the confectioners' sugar, vanilla, and milk. Drizzle the glaze over the tops of the cooled loaves before cutting into thick, yummy slices.

BAKER'S NOTE

For classic hot cross buns, after the dough has risen the first time, divide it into 12–16 equal pieces (depending on how big you want the buns to be) and roll each into a ball. Space the rolls out on a baking sheet lined with parchment and let rise until doubled. Bake until golden brown, about 18 minutes.

BACON, CARAMELIZED ONION, AND GRUYÈRE FOCACCIA

Rich with olive oil, nutty Gruyère cheese, crisp thick-cut bacon, and sweet onions, this focaccia is like taking a trip to the Alsace. The recipe is based on my brother's much-loved version, which he's been serving for years. Thanks Mark!

1 package (2¼ tsp) active dry yeast

2 tsp firmly packed light brown sugar

1 cup (8 fl oz/250 ml) warm water (110°F/43°C)

3 cups (15 oz/470 g) all-purpose flour

6 tbsp (3 fl oz/90 ml) olive oil, plus more for brushing

1 tsp kosher salt

1 tsp minced fresh rosemary

1 cup (4 oz/125 g) loosely packed shredded Gruyère cheese

6 slices thick-cut applewood-smoked bacon, chopped

2 yellow onions, halved and thinly sliced

makes 1 flatbread

BAKER'S NOTE

To use the focaccia for sandwiches, omit the onion and bacon toppings and shape the dough into a smaller, thicker rectangle or square. After it has cooled, cut into squares, split through the middle, and fill with goat cheese and grilled eggplant and peppers, or any of your other favorite sandwich fillings.

In the bowl of a stand mixer, dissolve the yeast and 1 teaspoon of the brown sugar in the warm water. Let stand until foamy, about 10 minutes. Add the flour, 4 tablespoons (2 fl oz/60 ml) of the oil, salt, rosemary, and cheese. Attach the dough hook and knead on medium-low speed until the dough is smooth and elastic, about 10 minutes. Form the dough into a ball, put it back into the bowl, and cover the bowl with plastic wrap. Let the dough rise in a warm, draft-free spot until it doubles, about 1 hour.

Meanwhile, in a large cast-iron frying pan, fry the bacon over medium-low heat until just crisp. Transfer to paper towels to drain. Discard all but a few teaspoons of the bacon fat. Add the onions and sauté over medium-low heat until they start to wilt, about 3 minutes. Stir in the remaining 1 teaspoon brown sugar and a pinch of salt and continue to cook until the onions are golden brown and caramelized, about 20 minutes. Remove from the heat, stir in the bacon, and let cool.

Oil a rimmed baking sheet with the remaining 2 tablespoons oil. Dump the dough onto the prepared pan and press it into a rough rectangle. Using your fingers, stretch the dough into a rectangle about 10 by 14 inches (25 by 35 cm). Cover the dough loosely with a kitchen towel and let rise in a warm, draft-free place until puffy, about 1 hour.

Position a rack in the middle of the oven and preheat to 425°F (220°C). Dimple the surface of the dough with your fingertips. Gently brush the dough with oil, then sprinkle evenly with the bacon-onion mixture. Bake until gorgeously golden, 15–18 minutes. Cut into squares and serve while warm.

A GOOD, HONEST
SANDWICH BREAD

Bread, for me, is one of the most soul-satisfying things you can bake. The aroma that permeates your house, the warm loaf fresh from the oven, the first slice you eat with a thick swipe of butter—it's the feeling and taste of home and all that is good in the world.

7 tbsp (3½ oz/105 g) unsalted butter

1 cup (8 fl oz/250 ml) whole milk

2½ tsp kosher salt

2¾ cups (11 oz/340 g) all-purpose flour, plus more as needed

2½ cups (12½ oz/390 g) white whole-wheat flour

1 package (2¼ tsp) instant yeast

1 tbsp sugar

makes 2 loaves

BAKER'S NOTE

This all-purpose, slightly wheaty loaf is both moist and lightly dense and is superb for anything from turkey or grilled cheese sandwiches to cinnamon toast and eggy French toast. You can turn it into an awesome white bread by using all-purpose flour only instead of adding wheat flour.

In a small saucepan, melt 6 tablespoons (3 oz/90 g) of the butter over low heat. Add the milk, 1 cup (8 fl oz/250 ml) water, and the salt, and stir until the mixture reaches 120°F (49°C). Remove from the heat.

In the bowl of a stand mixer fitted with the dough hook, combine the flours, yeast, and sugar and mix together on low speed. Add the melted butter mixture and mix together on low speed. Raise the speed to medium and knead until the dough is smooth, about 10 minutes, adding a little more all-purpose flour if needed for the dough to pull away from the sides of the bowl. The dough should be a little sticky.

Dump the dough onto a lightly floured work surface and knead for 1–2 minutes. Form the dough into a ball, place it in the mixing bowl, cover with plastic wrap, and let rise in a warm draft-free spot until doubled, about 1 hour.

Butter two 9-by-5-inch (23-by-13-cm) loaf pans. Dump the dough onto the lightly floured work surface. Divide into 2 equal pieces. Flatten each piece into an 8½-inch (21.5-cm) square. Roll up each piece of dough, pinch the seam to seal, and place the dough seam side down in a loaf pan. Cover with plastic wrap and let rise until puffy, about 45 minutes.

Position a rack in the middle of the oven and preheat to 375°F (190°C). Melt the remaining 1 tablespoon butter and gently brush the tops of each loaf with it. Bake until the loaves are golden brown and sound hollow when tapped, about 30 minutes. Turn out onto racks and let cool completely before slicing.

ANYTHING GOES PIZZA

This is a good, basic pizza recipe to try at home, and it makes for a fun pizza-making party (just double or triple the recipe). Experiment with different toppings, with or without the red sauce. Two of my favorite combinations are fontina and sautéed wild mushrooms, and red sauce drizzled with a little cream and topped with shaved Parmesan and cooked, crumbled spicy Italian sausage.

for the sponge
1 package (2¼ tsp) active dry yeast

1 cup (8 fl oz/250 ml) warm water (110°F/43°C)

1 cup (5 oz/155 g) bread flour

for the dough
3 cups (15 oz/470 g) bread flour

3 tbsp olive oil

2 tsp kosher salt

Semolina, cornmeal, or flour as needed

Olive oil for brushing

Pizza Sauce (page 215)

choice of toppings
crumbled, cooked Italian sausage; sliced *soppressata*; crumbled, cooked bacon; sautéed sliced mushrooms; sautéed spinach; caramelized onions; cooked artichoke hearts; roasted peppers; fresh basil leaves; pitted olives

1–1½ lb (16–24 oz/ 500–750 g) fresh mozzarella cheese, sliced

makes 3 pizzas

To make the sponge, in the bowl of a stand mixer, dissolve the yeast in the warm water and let stand until foamy, about 10 minutes. Whisk the flour into the yeast mixture. Cover the bowl with plastic wrap and let stand in a warm, draft-free place for about 4 hours or up to overnight. (I usually make the sponge the first thing in the morning or just before bed the night before.)

To make the dough, add the flour, olive oil, salt, and 1 cup (8 fl oz/ 250 ml) water to the sponge. Attach the dough hook and mix on medium-low speed until the ingredients are evenly mixed. Scrape down the sides of the bowl, then knead the dough for about 10 minutes. The dough will be quite sticky. Cover the bowl with plastic wrap and let the dough rise in a warm, draft-free place until doubled, about 2 hours, or let rise overnight in the refrigerator (bring the dough to room temperature before you form it).

Position a rack in the lower third of the oven. Put a pizza stone on the rack or line the rack with unglazed ceramic tiles. Preheat the oven to 500°F (260°C) for at least 30 minutes. (This step is important, as the stone or tiles need time to get really hot and absorb the heat; it's what will help make your crust crisp and chewy, as close as possible to the results from a professional pizza oven.)

Dump the dough onto a lightly floured work surface and divide into 3 equal balls. Set 2 balls aside and cover them with a damp kitchen towel. Flatten the third ball into a disk and use your fingers to stretch and press it out until it is as evenly thin as you can make it (it's a good idea to let the dough rest for about 5 minutes in the middle of all this tugging). Gently stretch the dough, rotating it as you stretch, until it is about 12 inches (30 cm) in diameter.

Dust a pizza peel with semolina. Place the dough round on the peel. Lightly brush it with olive oil. Spread a thin layer of sauce evenly on the dough, leaving a ½-inch (12-mm) border. Sprinkle on your toppings, then top with a third of the mozzarella slices. Slide the pizza onto the hot tiles or stone. Bake until the crust is golden brown and the toppings are sizzling, 7–10 minutes. Repeat to prepare and bake the remaining pizzas. Eat each pizza while bubbly and hot!

SOFT PRETZELS
WITH GRAINY MUSTARD

1 cup (8 fl oz/250 ml) warm water (110°F/43°C)

1 package (2¼ tsp) active dry yeast

1 tbsp sugar

3 tbsp olive oil, plus more if needed

3¼ cups (16½ oz/515 g) all-purpose flour

1 tsp kosher salt

⅓ cup (2½ oz/75 g) baking soda

Coarse salt for sprinkling

Grainy mustard for serving

makes 12 pretzels

In the bowl of a stand mixer, stir together the warm water, yeast, and sugar. Let stand until foamy, about 10 minutes. Add the 3 tablespoons oil, the flour, and kosher salt. Attach the dough hook and knead the dough on medium-low speed until smooth, about 10 minutes. Form the dough into a ball, cover the bowl with plastic wrap, and let rise in a warm, draft-free spot until doubled, about 1 hour.

Line 2 baking sheets with parchment paper and brush the parchment with oil. Dump the dough onto a lightly floured work surface, then cut it into 12 equal pieces. Roll each piece into a long rope about 18 inches (45 cm) long. With each rope positioned horizontally, bring the 2 ends up and toward the center as if forming an oval, cross one end over the other, and press each end into the bottom of the oval to create a pretzel shape. Place the pretzels on the prepared pan, spacing them evenly.

Position a rack in the middle of the oven and preheat to 450°F (230°C). Fill a large, wide saucepan with 7 cups (56 fl oz/1.75 l) water, stir in the baking soda, and bring to a boil. Gently drop 2 or 3 pretzels at a time into the boiling water (be careful not to overcrowd them). Boil for just under 1 minute, turning once with a large slotted spoon or spatula. Return the boiled pretzels to the baking sheet, top side up.

Sprinkle the pretzels with coarse salt. Bake until beautifully browned, about 10 minutes, rotating the pans about halfway through. Serve warm with big spoonfuls of grainy mustard.

If you really want to impress your friends at your next sports-inspired get-together, bake a batch of these guys. Be sure you eat them the same day you make them, preferably while they are still warm, as they don't keep well. But that shouldn't be a problem.

BAKER'S NOTE

The baking soda added to the boiling water makes a massive difference in these pretzels (trust me—I learned the hard way when testing this recipe). It's what helps them turn gorgeous and brown, so don't skip it.

CHAPTER THREE

COOKIES & BARS

WHOOPIE PIES
WITH SALTED DULCE DE LECHE

*Is it a pie? Is it a cake? Or is it a cookie?
I just like the name: Whoopie! Pie!
These superchocolatey, cakelike cookies
sandwich a gooey sweet and salty
caramel. The result is an überrich and
incredibly decadent dessert that
is positively addictive.*

for the cookies

6 tbsp (3 oz/90 g)
unsalted butter, at
room temperature

½ cup (3½ oz/105 g)
firmly packed light
brown sugar

1 large egg

1 tsp pure vanilla extract

¾ cup (4 oz/125 g)
all-purpose flour

½ cup (1½ oz/45 g)
natural cocoa powder

½ tsp baking soda

¼ tsp kosher salt

for the filling

4 tbsp (2 oz/60 g)
unsalted butter, at
room temperature

¾ cup (3 oz/90 g)
confectioners' sugar

2 tbsp heavy cream

¼–½ tsp kosher salt

⅓ cup (3 fl oz/80 ml)
dulce de leche

makes 10 whoopie pies

BAKER'S NOTE

Most upscale or Latin grocery stores carry jars
of *dulce de leche*, a thick caramel sauce made
from evaporated or sweetened milk that is
slowly simmered for a long period of time.

To make the cookies, in the bowl of a mixer fitted with the paddle attachment, beat the butter and sugar on medium-high speed until combined. Add the egg and vanilla and beat until blended. Sift the flour, cocoa, baking soda, and salt into the bowl and beat just until blended. Cover the bowl and refrigerate the dough until firm, about 2 hours.

Space 2 racks evenly in the oven and preheat to 350°F (180°C). Line 2 baking sheets with parchment.

With dampened hands, shape tablespoonfuls of the dough into balls. Place them firmly on the prepared pans, spacing them slightly apart and squishing them a little. You should have about 20 balls. Bake until the cookies are puffed and slightly firm, 8–10 minutes, rotating the pans about halfway through. Let the cookies cool on the pans for 5 minutes, then transfer to wire racks to cool completely.

While the cookies are cooling, make the filling: In the bowl of a mixer fitted with the paddle attachment, beat the butter and confectioners' sugar on medium-high speed until lightened. Stir in the cream and salt, to taste, on low speed, then stir in the *dulce de leche* until the filling is smooth.

Spread the flat side of half of the cookies with a big dollop of the filling. Top each with a second cookie, placing the flat side on the filling. (You'll probably have a bit more filling than you need, but if you're like me, you'll find a good use for it, and will sneak spoonfuls here and there.) Refrigerate until the filling is set, at least 1 hour. Whoopie!

PEANUT BUTTER–
CHOCOLATE SWIRLS

These crisp chocolate and peanut buttery cookies are great for a crowd, as one batch yields lots of cookies. Make the dough ahead and keep it in the freezer, then just slice and bake what you want.

1 cup (8 oz/250 g) unsalted butter, at room temperature

1½ cups (10½ oz/ 330 g) firmly packed light brown sugar

2 large eggs

1 cup (10 oz/315 g) good-quality unsweetened creamy peanut butter

1 tsp pure vanilla extract

2¼ cups (11½ oz/360 g) all-purpose flour

1 tsp baking soda

½ tsp kosher salt

1 bag (12 oz/375 g) semisweet chocolate chips

makes about 6 dozen cookies

BAKER'S NOTE

This is a soft dough, so you have to show it who's boss! Use the parchment to help you, and keep peeling it up and sprinkling it with flour if it gets too sticky. If you keep the dough floured, it will roll out more easily. When you spread the chocolate, brush off any excess flour, or the chocolate will be difficult to spread.

In the bowl of a mixer fitted with the paddle attachment, beat all but 1 tablespoon of the butter and the sugar on medium-high speed until lightened. Beat in the eggs one at a time, beating well after each addition. Beat in the peanut butter and vanilla until smooth. Sift the flour, baking soda, and salt into the bowl, and stir into the peanut butter mixture. Cover the bowl and refrigerate the dough for at least 30 minutes.

Meanwhile, in a heatproof bowl set over a saucepan filled with about an inch of water, melt the remaining 1 tablespoon butter with the chocolate chips over very low heat. Stir until smooth. Let cool slightly.

Divide the dough into 2 balls. Place 1 dough ball on a large piece of floured parchment paper. Flour the top of the dough, place another piece of parchment on top, and roll into a rectangle about 10 by 15 inches (25 by 38 cm). The dough should be about ⅛ inch (3 mm) thick. (See Note for tips on rolling out this dough.) Spread the rectangle with half of the chocolate mixture, leaving a 1-inch (2.5-cm) border on the long side closest to you. Starting from the long side farthest from you, and using the parchment to help, carefully roll the dough into a log. Place the log seam side down and wrap it in the parchment, twisting the ends to hold it tight. Repeat with the remaining dough and chocolate mixture. Refrigerate until firm, about 3 hours or ideally overnight.

Space 2 racks evenly in the oven and preheat to 350°F (180°C). Line 2 large baking sheets with parchment paper. Unwrap the logs, trim the ends of each log then cut crosswise into slices about ¼ inch (6 mm) thick. Space the cookies evenly on the prepared pans. You will need to bake in batches, so refrigerate the remaining portion of the logs until you are ready to cut and bake more cookies. Bake until the cookies are puffed and lightly golden, about 10 minutes, rotating the pans about halfway through. Let the cookies cool on the pans for 5 minutes, then transfer to wire racks to cool completely.

CHOCOLATE CRINKLE COOKIES

Chocolate, chocolate, and more chocolate. With a triple hit of bittersweet chocolate, cocoa powder, and chocolate chips, these melt-in-your-mouth brownielike cookies will make anyone's mouth water.

4 oz (125 g) bittersweet chocolate, chopped

6 tbsp (3 oz/90 g) unsalted butter

1½ cups (7½ oz/235 g) all-purpose flour

½ cup (1½ oz/45 g) natural cocoa powder

1 tsp baking powder

½ tsp baking soda

½ tsp kosher salt

4 large eggs

1½ cups (12 oz/375 g) granulated sugar

1 tsp pure vanilla extract

1 cup (5 oz/150 g) mini semisweet chocolate chips

½ cup (2 oz/60 g) confectioners' sugar

makes about 2½ dozen cookies

BAKER'S NOTE

When baking cookies on multiple sheets, space two racks evenly in the oven and then switch and rotate the pans about halfway through baking. This will ensure even cooking.

Place the chocolate and butter in a small saucepan over very low heat and stir until melted. Don't walk away—you don't want the chocolate to burn. Let cool slightly. In a bowl, sift together the flour, cocoa, baking powder, baking soda, and salt.

In the bowl of a mixer fitted with the paddle attachment, beat the eggs, granulated sugar, and vanilla on high speed until thick and fluffy, about 3 minutes. Stir in the melted chocolate mixture on low speed, then add the dry ingredients and stir until incorporated. Stir in the chocolate chips. Cover the bowl and refrigerate the dough until it is firm enough to roll into balls, about 2 hours.

Space 2 racks evenly in the oven and preheat to 325°F (165°C). Line 2 baking sheets with parchment paper. Sift the confectioners' sugar into a small bowl.

Roll heaping tablespoonfuls of dough into balls, then roll each in the confectioners' sugar. Place the balls on the prepared pans, spacing them slightly apart and squishing them down slightly to flatten them and keep them in place.

Bake until the cookies are puffed and crinkled, about 15 minutes, rotating the baking sheets about halfway through. Let the cookies cool on the pans for 5 minutes, then transfer to wire racks to cool completely.

CINNAMON-OATMEAL COOKIES

Crisp and chewy and spiked with cinnamon, these cookies are one of my go-to treats from childhood. For some, an oatmeal cookie is not an oatmeal cookie without juicy raisins, but I prefer tiny, plump dried currants, or better yet, gooey chocolate chips.

1½ cups (7½ oz/235 g) all-purpose flour

1 tsp baking soda

2 tsp ground cinnamon

½ tsp kosher salt

¾ cup (6 oz/185 g) unsalted butter, at room temperature

1 cup (7 oz/220 g) firmly packed light brown sugar

½ cup (4 oz/125 g) granulated sugar

2 large eggs

2 tsp pure vanilla extract

2¼ cups (7 oz/220 g) old-fashioned rolled oats

1 cup (6 oz/185 g) dried currants, raisins, or chocolate chips (optional)

makes about 2½ dozen cookies

Space 2 racks evenly in the oven and preheat to 350°F (180°C). Line 2 baking sheets with parchment paper.

In a bowl, sift together the flour, baking soda, cinnamon, and salt. In the bowl of a mixer fitted with the paddle attachment, beat the butter and sugars on medium-high speed until combined. Add the eggs and vanilla and beat until well blended. Add the dry ingredients and oats and beat on low speed until incorporated. Stir in the currants, if using.

Drop heaping teaspoonfuls of dough onto the prepared pans, spacing them slightly apart. Bake until the cookies are golden brown, about 15 minutes, rotating the pans halfway through. Let the cookies cool on the pans for 5 minutes, then transfer to wire racks to cool completely.

BAKER'S NOTE

To ensure crisp bottoms, don't let your cookies sit on the baking sheet for too long after they've come out of the oven. After the cookies have cooled for a few minutes, transfer them to a wire rack to cool (for as long as you can keep your hands off them).

SUGAR MAMA'S
BAKESHOP
AUSTIN, TEXAS

Sugar Mama's Bakeshop is a cheery bakery located in the heart of Texas. Committed to the local community, they use the highest quality ingredients in all of their from-scratch recipes, producing delicious baked goods that are renowned throughout Austin.

WHO IS SUGAR MAMA?

I am! Originally when the name was conceived it was a sweet name that my friends and family fell in love with. After the shop opened, a man came in one day and said "you must be Sugar Mama." From that point on, I was THE Sugar Mama.

WHAT'S YOUR FAVORITE FLAVOR?

Chocolate cake with chocolate frosting, hands down. I do love desserts equally, but chocolate holds a special place in my heart.

WHAT'S IN THE OVEN RIGHT NOW?

Our seasonal cupcake is a butter cake with butter pecan frosting and candied jalapeños. We also have our seasonal dessert bar: Hello P'Nut, which features semisweet and milk chocolate, along with honey roasted peanuts, and peanut butter chips.

WHAT'S YOUR FAVORITE FOOD TREND?

We're a hundred percent on board with the eating-local-whenever-possible movement. I hope it's not just a trend, but focusing on fresh local ingredients is better for our families, and the planet. At our farmers' market, you can get everything from locally made mustard and pickles, to staples like eggs and bread. Locally produced items are always more flavorful as they're usually in season.

TUESDAY
PISTACHIO CHOCOLATE CHIP
THE ODD COUPLE · ELVIS
STRAWBERRY LOVE
FRIDA

WEDNESDAY
PEANUT BUTTER CUP (CAKE)
CHERRY LIMEADE · THE
LITTLE MONKEY · GERMAN
CHOC · JOYFUL ALMOND

THURSDAY
THE HULA · PB & HONEY
CHURCHILL · MUD PIE
BANANA PUDDIN'

FRIDAY
THE ODD COUPLE · ELVIS
PINA COLADA · BLACK & TAN
ROOT BEER FLOAT

SATURDAY
THE HEMINGWAY · FRIDA
PEANUT BUTTER CUP (CAKE)
FRENCH TOAST

SUNDAY
MUD PIE

SMORES BAR
HOUSEMADE MARSHMALLOW · FUDGE
FILLING & GRAHAM CRACKER CRUST

SXSWEET
Pecan

COOKIES 1.25 13 DOZ
OATMEAL · BUTTERSCOTCH · ICED MOLASSES
MILK CHOCOLATE CHIP · Everything

SIGNATURE
SUGAR COOKIE 2.25

SUGAR MAMA'S BAKESHOP
RASPBERRY LINZER BARS
WITH ALMOND GLAZE

A thick layer of juicy fresh raspberries are spread over a sugary crust, then topped with streusel-like crumbles and sweet almond glaze, making these absolutely decadent. For thicker bars, use a 9-inch baking pan and for a thinner version, use a 10-inch pan.

for the crust

3 cups (15 oz/470 g) all-purpose flour

¾ cup (6 oz/185 g) granulated sugar

¾ cup (6 oz/185 g) firmly packed brown sugar

½ tsp kosher salt

Grated zest of 1 lemon

1½ cups (12 oz/375 g) cold unsalted butter, cut into chunks

for the filling

4 cups (1 lb/500 g) raspberries

⅓ cup (3 oz/90 g) granulated sugar

1 tbsp cornstarch

for the glaze

1½ cups (6 oz/180 g) sifted confectioners' sugar

5 tbsp (3 fl oz/80 ml) heavy cream

½ tsp pure almond extract

makes about 12 bars

Position a rack in the middle of the oven and preheat to 350°F (180°C). Butter an 9- or 10-inch (23- or 25-cm) square baking pan.

To make the crust, in a bowl, combine the flour, granulated and brown sugars, salt, and lemon zest. Add the butter and, using a pastry blender or 2 table knives, cut into the flour mixture until the butter is the size of small peas.

Transfer three-fourths of the crust mixture to the prepared pan and press firmly to make an even layer on the bottom and slightly up the sides. Bake until golden brown, about 15 minutes. Set the crust aside to cool while you make the filling. Chill the remainder of the crust mixture in the refrigerator.

To make the filling, in a saucepan, stir together the raspberries, granulated sugar, and cornstarch. Simmer over medium heat, stirring often, until the sugar dissolves and the berries are juicy but not completely broken down, about 2 minutes. Transfer to a bowl and let cool.

Spread the filling over the partially baked crust. Crumble the chilled crust mixture over the filling. Bake until golden and bubbly, about 25 minutes. Let cool completely in the pan on a wire rack.

To make the glaze, in a bowl, combine the confectioners' sugar, cream, and almond extract. Whisk the ingredients together until combined. Fit a piping bag with a small, plain tip, and fill it with the glaze. Pipe over the top in a crisscross pattern. Refrigerate until chilled, at least 1 hour. Cut into bars.

CHOCOLATE CHIP COOKIES WITH ALMONDS AND ORANGE ZEST

My dad loves chocolate chip cookies. He'll almost always choose this crisp-chewy classic, oozing with semisweet chocolate, over just about any other sweet. I've taken these a step beyond the usual by adding a hint of orange zest and some toasty almonds.

1 cup (8 oz/250 g) unsalted butter, at room temperature

⅔ cup (5 oz/155 g) granulated sugar

⅔ cup (5 oz/155 g) firmly packed light brown sugar

Finely grated zest of 1 large orange

2 large eggs

2 tsp pure vanilla extract

2⅓ cups (12 oz/375 g) all-purpose flour

1 tsp baking soda

1 tsp kosher salt

1 bag (12 oz/375 g) semisweet chocolate chips

1 cup (4½ oz/140 g) slivered almonds, lightly toasted (page 15)

makes about 3 dozen cookies

Space 2 racks evenly in the oven and preheat to 350°F (180°C). Line 2 baking sheets with parchment paper.

In the bowl of a mixer fitted with the paddle attachment, beat the butter on medium-high speed until fluffy. Add the sugars and orange zest and beat until the mixture is well combined. Add the eggs and vanilla and beat until blended. Sift the flour, baking soda, and salt into the bowl and mix on low speed just until blended. Stir in the chocolate chips and almonds until blended.

Drop heaping tablespoonfuls of the dough onto the prepared pans, spacing them slightly apart. Bake until the cookies are golden brown around the edges, 10–12 minutes. I usually rotate the pans after 5 minutes. Let the cookies cool on the pans for 5 minutes, then transfer to wire racks to cool completely (although these taste awesome when they are gooey and warm).

BAKER'S NOTE

For a classic chocolate chip cookie, omit the orange zest and almonds. If you like your cookies chewier, take them out of the oven a few minutes early. For crisp-all-the-way-through cookies, continue to bake them a few minutes longer.

TOASTY ALMOND MERINGUES

If you think you don't like meringues, try these. The toasted almonds help temper the sweetness, balancing out the flavor beautifully. Not only that, but these are a great bet for anyone on a gluten-free diet.

4 large eggs	1 cup (7 oz/220 g) superfine sugar
1½ cups (6 oz/185 g) sliced almonds, toasted (page 15)	1 tsp pure vanilla extract
½ tsp cream of tartar	makes about 3½ dozen meringues
Pinch of kosher salt	

BAKER'S NOTE

To whip up the fluffiest egg whites, start with a clean mixing bowl and whisk; any fat or grease will impede the fluff factor. Room-temperature or warm egg whites are best. Be sure to add cream of tartar, which helps stabilize the whites. Finally, don't overwhip the whites, or they will turn grainy.

Position a rack in the middle of the oven and preheat to 300°F (150°C). Line 2 baking sheets with parchment paper.

Separate the eggs while they are cold; reserve the yolks for another use. Put the egg whites in a bowl. Fill another, larger bowl about halfway with very hot water. Place the bowl with the egg whites in the hot water and swirl the whites with a whisk to warm them for a few minutes (warm egg whites are more stable and will whip higher than cold egg whites). Meanwhile, finely chop the almonds.

Remove the egg whites from the bowl of hot water, and add the cream of tartar and salt. Using a mixer fitted with the whip attachment, beat the egg whites on medium-high speed until foamy. Increase the speed to high and add the sugar a little at a time, beating until stiff, glossy peaks form. Beat in the vanilla. Using a rubber spatula, gently fold in the chopped almonds. Drop heaping teaspoonfuls of the meringue onto the prepared pans, spacing them apart. You can also pipe the meringues onto the baking sheet using a pastry bag and a wide plain tip.

Bake until the meringues are lightly colored and puffed, about 20 minutes. Turn off the oven and prop the door open with a wooden spoon. Let the meringues dry out slightly and cool completely, about 2 hours, before popping them into your mouth.

CHEWY GINGER-MOLASSES COOKIES

Studded with hunks of crystallized ginger, these spicy cookies are crisp as well as chewy. They would make great ice-cream sandwiches: simply squish a small scoop of softened vanilla ice cream between two cookies and have at it.

2 cups (10 oz/315 g) all-purpose flour

1½ tsp baking soda

½ tsp kosher salt

1 tsp ground ginger

1 tsp ground cinnamon

¼ tsp ground allspice

¾ cup (6 oz/185 g) unsalted butter, at room temperature

1 cup (7 oz/220 g) firmly packed light brown sugar

1 large egg

½ cup (5½ oz/170 g) molasses

⅓–½ cup (2–3 oz/ 60–90 g) chopped crystallized ginger

makes about 2½ dozen cookies

Space 2 racks evenly in the oven and preheat to 350°F (180°C). Line 2 baking sheets with parchment paper.

In a bowl, sift together the flour, baking soda, salt, ginger, cinnamon, and allspice. In the bowl of a mixer fitted with the paddle attachment, beat the butter and sugar on medium-high speed until creamy. Add the egg and molasses and beat until smooth. Add the dry ingredients and crystallized ginger and beat on low speed until incorporated.

Drop tablespoonfuls of the dough onto the prepared pans, spacing them slightly apart (they will spread out a bit). Bake until the cookies are golden brown, about 12 minutes, rotating the pans about halfway through. Let the cookies cool on the pans for 5 minutes, then transfer to wire racks to cool completely.

BAKER'S NOTE

To make measuring thick, sticky molasses easier, lightly spray the measuring pitcher with cooking spray before pouring in the molasses. It will glide right out!

CINNAMON-SUGAR ROLL-UPS

For as long as I can remember, this is what I've done with the leftover scraps of dough from making pies. As kids, my brother and I were in charge of making these rolled-up cookies. We never measured a thing, opting instead to wing it, and sometimes experimented with other fillings, like a smear of jam or melted chocolate chips.

for the dough	for the filling
½ cup (4 oz/125 g) unsalted butter, at room temperature	2½ tsp ground cinnamon
4 oz (125 g) cream cheese, at room temperature	½ cup (4 oz/125 g) sugar
¼ cup (2 fl oz/60 ml) heavy cream	3 tbsp unsalted butter, at room temperature
1⅔ cups (8½ oz/265 g) all-purpose flour	1 large egg beaten with 1 tsp warm water
¼ tsp kosher salt	makes 2 dozen roll-ups

BAKER'S NOTE

To turn these into jam-filled or chocolate-filled roll-ups, use about ⅓ cup (3 oz/90 g) of your favorite jam or ⅓ cup (3 fl oz/80 ml) melted chocolate chips in place of the cinnamon-sugar and softened butter. Spread the jam or chocolate evenly over the dough, and roll and bake as directed.

To make the dough, in a food processor, combine the butter, cream cheese, and cream and process until smooth. Add the flour and salt and process until the dough starts to come together. Dump the dough onto a well-floured work surface. Knead a few times, then divide it in half, form 2 disks, and wrap each disk in plastic wrap. Refrigerate the dough for at least 30 minutes.

Position a rack in the middle of the oven and preheat to 375°F (190°C). Line a baking sheet with parchment paper.

On a lightly floured work surface, roll out 1 dough disk into a rectangle about 7 by 20 inches (18 by 50 cm).

To make the filling, in a small bowl, stir together the cinnamon and sugar. Spread the dough with half of the butter, leaving a narrow border uncovered on the long side nearest you; use a gentle touch (you can spread the butter with your fingers) so you don't tear the dough. Sprinkle half of the cinnamon-sugar mixture over the butter. Starting at the long side farthest from you, roll up the dough into a log. Turn the log so that the seam is down, then press to seal. Trim the ends. Cut the log crosswise into 12 equal slices, each about 1¼ inches (3 cm) wide. Lightly brush with the egg wash. Place the slices on one half of the prepared pan, spacing them evenly, and repeat the steps with the remaining dough disk and filling.

Bake until the roll-ups are golden brown and the filling is oozing a bit, about 20 minutes. Let cool slightly before eating (not that I can ever wait—I always burn my tongue, as I can't resist tasting these right out of the oven).

HONEYED BISCOTTI
WITH ALMONDS AND DATES

You'll want to bake these for the incredible aroma that will permeate your house and have you salivating. Biscotti take a bit of time and effort, but these are well worth it: crisp but not brittle with a honeyed sweetness that is balanced nicely with the toasted almonds and orange zest. They are perfect for dunking in your afternoon espresso.

2 cups (10 oz/315 g)
all-purpose flour

1 tsp baking powder

¼ tsp baking soda

⅛ tsp kosher salt

2 large eggs

½ cup (4 fl oz/125 ml)
canola oil

⅔ cup (8 oz/250 g)
honey

⅓ cup (3 oz/90 g)
sugar

1 tsp pure vanilla extract

Finely grated zest
of 1 orange

1 cup (5½ oz/170 g)
salted, roasted whole
almonds, roughly
chopped

1 cup (6 oz/185 g) dates,
halved lengthwise,
pitted, and roughly
chopped

1 large egg white beaten
with 1 tsp water

makes about 4 dozen
biscotti

In a bowl, sift together the flour, baking powder, baking soda, and salt. In a large bowl, whisk together the eggs, oil, honey, sugar, vanilla, and zest. Add the dry ingredients and stir to combine. Stir in the almonds and dates. Cover the bowl and refrigerate the dough for at least 2 hours.

Position a rack in the middle of the oven and preheat to 350°F (180°C). Line 2 baking sheets with parchment paper.

Divide the dough in half. With wet hands, shape each portion into a long, thin log about 15 inches (38 cm) long and 2 inches (5 cm) wide. Place the logs on one of the prepared pans, spacing them evenly (they will spread quite a bit). Brush the tops and sides lightly with the egg wash. Bake until golden, about 20 minutes. Let cool for about 15 minutes.

Cut the logs crosswise into slices about ½ inch (12 mm) thick. Carefully lay the slices, cut side down, on the prepared pans. Space 2 oven racks evenly in the oven and reduce the temperature to 325°F (165°C). Bake the biscotti until toasted and crisp, about 15 minutes, turning the biscotti once and rotating the baking sheets about halfway through. Let the biscotti cool on the pans for 5 minutes, then transfer to wire racks to cool completely.

BAKER'S NOTE

Make sure to chill the dough so that it firms a bit before shaping the logs. Wetting your hands before working with a sticky dough also helps ensure that you don't stick to it.

BUTTERSCOTCH BLONDIES

This is the real deal...no butterscotch chips here! You might not make it past the yummy butterscotch sauce; you can easily stop there and drizzle the sauce over vanilla ice cream for a decadent indulgence. But these gooey, rich treats make it worth seeing the recipe through to the end.

½ cup (4 oz/125 g) unsalted butter

2 cups (12 oz/370 g) lightly packed dark brown sugar

1 cup (8 fl oz/250 ml) heavy cream

2 tsp pure vanilla extract

2 tbsp dark rum

1 tsp kosher salt

2 cups (10 oz/315 g) all-purpose flour

1 tsp baking powder

2 large eggs

Confectioners' sugar for dusting (optional)

makes about 2 dozen blondies

In a saucepan, melt the butter over medium heat. Using a heatproof rubber spatula, stir in the brown sugar and cook until the sugar starts bubbling like molten lava, about 4 minutes. Reduce the heat to medium-low, stir in the cream, and let it bubble away, stirring with a big whisk, until smooth and slightly thickened, about 10 minutes. Stir in the vanilla, rum, and salt. Let cool to room temperature.

Position a rack in the middle of the oven and preheat to 350°F (180°C). Generously butter a 9-inch (23-cm) square baking dish.

In a bowl, whisk together the flour and baking powder. Stir the butterscotch mixture into the dry ingredients, then whisk in the eggs one at a time, beating well after each addition.

Spread the batter into the prepared dish and bake until a toothpick inserted into the center comes out relatively clean, 15–18 minutes. Let cool completely in the dish, then cut into squares or bars. Dust with confectioners' sugar before serving, if desired.

BAKER'S NOTE

The blondies can be embellished further with about 1 cup (6 oz/185 g) semisweet chocolate chips or white chocolate chunks added to the batter. Or go crazy with a mixture of both.

COCONUT-LIME
SHORTBREAD

A good shortbread cookie should be buttery and tender, crumbly and toothsome. This recipe takes the classic version and gives it a Caribbean twist with sweet toasted coconut and zesty lime.

¾ cup (6 oz/185 g) unsalted butter, at room temperature

⅓ cup (3 oz/90 g) sugar, plus more for sprinkling

Finely grated zest of 1 large lime

½ tsp kosher salt

⅓ cup (1½ oz/45 g) packed sweetened shredded coconut, lightly toasted (page 15)

1⅓ cups (7 oz/220 g) all-purpose flour

makes about 2 dozen cookies

BAKER'S NOTE

Butter is an essential part of shortbread, and its flavor should come through in the finished cookie. Be sure to use the best-quality, freshest butter you can when making these cookies.

In the bowl of a mixer fitted with the paddle attachment, beat the butter and ⅓ cup sugar on medium-high speed until combined. Add the lime zest and salt, then stir in the coconut and flour. Beat on low speed until the dough comes together. Dump the dough onto a large piece of parchment paper, top with another large piece of parchment, and roll out the dough about ¼ inch (6 mm) thick. Put the parchment-covered dough on a baking sheet and refrigerate for about 30 minutes.

Position a rack in the middle of the oven and preheat the oven to 325°F (165°C). Slide the dough onto a work surface. Remove the top piece of parchment and use it to line the baking sheet.

Cut the dough into finger-sized rectangles about 1 inch (2.5 cm) wide or use a cookie cutter to cut into shapes. Transfer to the baking sheet, spacing the dough pieces slightly apart. Pierce the surface of the dough all over with a fork and sprinkle with sugar. Bake until lightly golden at the edges, about 22 minutes. Let the cookies cool on the pan for 5 minutes, then transfer to a wire rack to cool completely.

PISTACHIO-ALMOND BARS
WITH CITRUS GLAZE

These sweet-and-salty bars were inspired by a much-loved cake recipe from one of my favorite authors, Nigel Slater. The citrus glaze helps highlight the toasty flavor of the pistachios and almonds, making these bars an ideal option for anyone who isn't crazy about sweets that are too sweet.

Finely grated zest and juice of 1 orange

Finely grated zest and juice of 1 lemon

1 cup (4 oz/125 g) unsalted, shelled pistachios

1 cup (4½ oz/140 g) slivered almonds

¾ cup (6 oz/185 g) granulated sugar

¾ cup (4 oz/125 g) all-purpose flour

1 tsp baking powder

½ tsp kosher salt

¾ cup (6 oz/185 g) unsalted butter, at room temperature

3 large eggs

2 cups (8 oz/250 g) confectioners' sugar

makes about 18 bars

Position a rack in the middle of the oven and preheat to 350°F (180°C). Generously butter a 7½-by-12-inch (19-by-30-cm) or 9-by-13-inch (23-by-33-cm) baking dish and dust with flour.

Strain the orange and lemon juices into a bowl, then measure out 3 tablespoons and place in a separate bowl. You should have about ⅓ cup (3 fl oz/80 ml) citrus juice remaining (if not, add a bit more orange or lemon juice).

In a food processor, pulse the nuts, the citrus zests, and half of the granulated sugar until finely ground. Put in a bowl and stir in the flour, baking powder, and salt. In a mixer fitted with the paddle attachment, beat the butter and remaining sugar on medium-high speed until light and fluffy. Add the eggs one at a time, mixing well after each addition. Add the reserved ⅓ cup citrus juice. Gently stir in the nut mixture just until combined.

Spread the batter in the prepared dish. Bake until light golden brown, about 30 minutes. Let cool in the dish for about 20 minutes, then turn out onto a wire rack set over a baking sheet to cool completely.

Stir the confectioners' sugar into the 3 tablespoons citrus juice, then pour over the top and spread evenly. Let the glaze set for about 30 minutes before cutting into bars.

BAKER'S NOTE

The best tool for zesting citrus is a fine-toothed Microplane grater, which allows you to get all the good stuff—the colorful rind and the citrus oil—without any of the bitter white pith. If you don't have one handy, use a vegetable peeler to remove only the colored part of the peel (the zest) and then finely mince it.

SMITTEN KITCHEN
PEACH–BROWN BUTTER SHORTBREAD

This contemporary twist on classic buttery shortbread celebrates summer's beloved bounty of peaches. Whether you pick them off a tree or buy them at the market, for the best results, choose the juiciest, most fragrant, and ripest peaches that you can get your hands on.

1 cup (8 oz/250 g) cold unsalted butter

1 cup (8 oz/250 g) granulated sugar

1 tsp baking powder

2¾ cups (14 oz/440 g) all-purpose flour

¼ tsp ground cinnamon

⅛ tsp freshly grated nutmeg

¼ tsp kosher salt

1 large egg

2 juicy, ripe but slightly firm peaches, pitted and thinly sliced

makes about 2 dozen squares

DEB PERELMAN
WWW.SMITTENKITCHEN.COM

Deb Perelman doesn't bother with fancy ingredients or time-consuming techniques. Instead, she focuses on creating easy recipes made from scratch in her tiny New York City apartment. A reporter by day, she spends her free time sharing her love of food through her wildly popular blog, Smitten Kitchen, where you'll find her recipe arsenal of "comfort foods stepped up a bit." Look for yummy re-creations such as homemade Oreo cookies and Goldfish crackers.

In a saucepan, melt the butter over medium-low heat. The melted butter will foam, then become clear golden, and finally start to turn brown and smell nutty. Stir frequently, scraping up any bits from the bottom. Watch the butter carefully at the end, as it turns brown quickly. Chill in the freezer until solid but not completely frozen, about 30 minutes.

Position a rack in the middle of the oven and preheat to 375°F (190°C). Butter a 9-by-13-inch (23-by-33-cm) baking pan.

In a bowl, whisk together the sugar, baking powder, flour, cinnamon, nutmeg, and salt. Using a pastry blender or 2 table knives, blend the solidified brown butter and the egg into the dry ingredients. The brown butter mixture will be crumbly. Pat three-fourths of the mixture into the bottom of the prepared pan, pressing firmly. Arrange the peach slices on top in a single layer. Crumble the remaining brown butter mixture evenly over the peaches.

Bake until the top is slightly brown and you can see a little color around the edges, about 30 minutes. Let cool completely in the pan, then cut into squares.

S'MORES BROWNIES

Within this recipe is a fantastic brownie— just the right balance of fudgy and cakey with a crackle top—embellished with crunchy graham crackers and big melting marshmallows. If you'd prefer the classic, just leave those two ingredients out and bake as directed.

1 cup (8 oz/250 g) unsalted butter

10 oz (315 g) bittersweet chocolate, finely chopped

1 cup (8 oz/250 g) granulated sugar

¾ cup (6 oz/185 g) firmly packed light brown sugar

4 large eggs

2 tsp pure vanilla extract

1 tsp kosher salt

1⅓ cups (5½ oz/170 g) cake flour

3 tbsp natural cocoa powder

About 6 graham crackers, roughly crushed with your hands

About 12 jumbo marshmallows

makes 12 brownies

Position a rack in the middle of the oven and preheat to 350°F (180°C). Generously butter a 9-by-13-inch (23-by-33-cm) baking dish.

In a saucepan, melt the butter and chocolate over low heat, stirring often, about 4 minutes. Remove from the heat and whisk in the sugars. Whisk in the eggs one at a time, beating well after each addition. Whisk in the vanilla and salt.

Sift the flour and cocoa over the chocolate mixture and, using a rubber spatula, stir in until just blended. Stir in the graham crackers. Pour into the prepared dish and spread evenly. Top evenly with the marshmallows.

Bake until a toothpick inserted into the center comes out almost completely clean, 30–35 minutes. Let cool in the dish on a wire rack, then cut into big, gooey squares.

BAKER'S NOTE

To make it easier to cut the brownies, fill a tall glass with very hot water and have a paper towel handy. Dip your knife in the water and wipe it off before each cut. This works great for cutting anything sticky, such as frosted layer cakes or cookie bars.

LEMONY COOKIE POPS

¾ cup (6 oz/185 g) unsalted butter, at room temperature

¾ cup (6 oz/185 g) granulated sugar

1 heaping, tightly packed tbsp finely grated lemon zest

1 tsp pure vanilla extract

1 large egg

1 large egg yolk

2 cups (10 oz/315 g) all-purpose flour

½ tsp kosher salt

24 lollipop sticks

for the glaze

1 cup (4 oz/125 g) confectioners' sugar

2 tbsp lemon juice

Sprinkles, food coloring, or other decorations (see Note; optional)

makes about 2 dozen cookies

In the bowl of a mixer fitted with the paddle attachment, beat the butter and granulated sugar on medium-high speed until creamy. Add the zest, vanilla, egg, and egg yolk and beat until smooth. Add the flour and salt and beat on low speed until the crumbly dough comes together. Cover the bowl and refrigerate the dough until chilled and firm, about 2 hours.

Space 2 racks evenly in the oven and preheat to 350°F (180°C). Line 2 baking sheets with parchment paper.

On a lightly floured work surface, roll out the dough ¼ inch (6 mm) thick. Using a 3-inch (7.5-cm) flower-shaped or fluted cutter, cut out cookies. Insert a stick into each one, pushing it about midway through. Use a spatula to put the cookies on the prepared pans, spacing them slightly apart (you might need to bake the cookies in batches).

Bake until the cookies are very lightly golden, 10–12 minutes, rotating the pans about halfway through. Let the cookies cool on the pans for at least 15 minutes, then transfer to wire racks to cool completely.

To make the glaze, in a bowl, stir together the confectioners' sugar and lemon juice until smooth. You can separate it into different bowls and add food coloring if you want to get fancy. Smear the glaze on the cookies and decorate with sprinkles or designs (see Note), if desired.

BAKER'S NOTE

If you want to get fancy, pull out your piping bag to make fun decorations on the cookies. Make the glaze with about half the lemon juice, adding a bit more as needed until you get a nice thick consistency. Load up the bag, fitted with a small, thin tip, and pipe away.

The first time I made these, they were for an embellishment to a "dirt cake"—chocolate cake and whipped cream topped with crushed Oreo cookies layered in a clean flowerpot. But they are also supercute on their own.

MICHELLE GAYER
SALTY TART
MINNEAPOLIS, MINNESOTA

With experience in some of the country's best bakeries, nationally acclaimed pastry chef Michelle Gayer has brought her talent and skill to her own shop, the Salty Tart Bakery. The beloved bakery's arsenal of sweet and savory pastries, fresh breads, and cakes has left an indelible mark on the Twin Cities food scene.

WHAT'S THE BEST PART ABOUT MAKING PASTRIES AND BREADS?
The smells! Nothing is better than the dreamy and intoxicating smells wafting off freshly baked goods.

WHAT MAKES YOUR BAKERY UNIQUE?
We only have 400 square feet, and the amount of people and product that go through the bakery any day is absolutely mind blowing!

SWEET OR SAVORY?
Savory for sure. It's just sweet, sweet, sweet all day, so we make it a priority to have savories as much as possible.

WHAT'S YOUR FAVORITE THING TO EAT?
Young pastry cooks!

WHAT DESSERT WOULD YOU BRING TO A DESSERT ISLAND?
An Icee: three-fourths cherry with a splash of Coke.

SALTY TART
Bakery

SALTY TART
CHEWY CHOCOLATE MERINGUES

Crunchy on the outside and gooey on the inside, these gems are not only a cinch to make but completely addictive—you won't be able to stop at one (or two or three). The cocoa nibs add a nice crunch and nutty flavor, but if you can't find them, don't worry, they can be left out.

1 cup (8 fl oz/250 ml) large egg whites (about 7)

2 cups (1 lb/500 g) sugar

5 tbsp (1 oz/30 g) natural cocoa powder

4 oz (125 g) bittersweet chocolate, finely chopped

4 oz (125 g) cocoa nibs

makes about 2 dozen meringues

Space 2 racks evenly in the middle of the oven and preheat to 350°F (180°C). Line 2 baking sheets with parchment paper.

In a clean, dry, heatproof bowl, whisk together the egg whites and sugar. Set over (but not touching) simmering water in a saucepan. Whisk constantly until the sugar is completely dissolved. Remove from the heat.

Using a mixer fitted with the whip attachment, beat the eggs on high speed until stiff and glossy. Sift the cocoa over the meringue. Sprinkle with the chocolate and the cocoa nibs, then fold together gently with a rubber spatula until combined.

Drop the meringue by heaping tablespoons, spaced slightly apart, onto the prepared baking sheets. Bake for 9 minutes. Rotate the pans and bake until the cookies are fluffy, full of cracks, and spring back when touched, about 9 minutes. Carefully pick up the parchment sheets and transfer the cookies, still on the parchment, to wire racks to cool.

OATMEAL JAMMY BARS

The great thing about these crave-worthy bars is that you only have to make one dough. Part of it is pressed into the pan bottom for the crust, and the rest serves as the crunchy streusel topping. Sandwiched in between is your favorite tart-sweet jam.

1⅔ cups (8½ oz/265 g) all-purpose flour

1 cup (7 oz/220 g) firmly packed light brown sugar

½ tsp kosher salt

¼ tsp baking soda

1 tsp ground cinnamon

2 tsp pure vanilla extract

Finely grated zest of 1 small orange

¾ cup (6 oz/185 g) cold unsalted butter, cut into chunks

1⅔ cups (5 oz/155 g) old-fashioned rolled oats

1½ cups (15 oz/470 g) of your favorite jam, such as apricot or raspberry, or a mixture

makes about 18 bars

Position a rack in the middle of the oven and preheat to 350°F (180°C). Generously butter a 9-by-13-inch (23-by-33-cm) baking dish.

In a food processor, combine the flour, sugar, salt, baking soda, cinnamon, vanilla, orange zest, and butter. Pulse until the mixture looks like chunky crumbs. Add the oats and pulse a few times to mix. Press about two-thirds of the oat mixture into the bottom of the prepared pan. The dough will be super crumbly, and you might wonder if it will ever bake together, but press it down firmly so it all squishes together. I assure you that it will work. Spread the jam evenly over the top, then sprinkle the remaining oat mixture over the jam.

Bake until the top is golden brown and you can see the jam bubbling, 35–40 minutes. Let cool in the dish, then cut into bars.

BAKER'S NOTE

I love making and canning jam, and it's something I do nearly every summer when I can't keep up with the plums and cherry tomatoes in my backyard. This is a good way to use any flavor of homemade fruit jam that you have on hand.

KEY LIME
PIE BARS

The thing I remember most about my grandmother, besides that she played bridge and had a jug of moonshine in her pantry, was that she made the best key lime pie. Her version was not at all traditional—you wouldn't find any sweetened condensed milk in her pie. These bars are an homage to her.

for the crust

6 oz (185 g) graham crackers (about 11 crackers)

¼ cup (2 oz/60 g) granulated sugar

Pinch of kosher salt

6 tbsp (3 oz/90 g) unsalted butter, melted

for the filling

3 large eggs

2 large egg yolks

¾ cup (6 oz/185 g) granulated sugar

Pinch of kosher salt

2 tsp finely grated Key lime or lime zest

½ cup Key lime or lime juice

½ cup (4 oz/125 g) sour cream

3 tbsp all-purpose flour

Confectioners' sugar or Whipped Cream (page 214) for serving

makes about 10 bars

Position a rack in the middle of the oven and preheat to 350°F (180°C). Lightly butter a 7½-by-12-inch (19-by-30-cm) baking dish (a 9-inch/23-cm square dish will work fine, too). Line the dish with a piece of parchment paper large enough to overhang the sides. Press the parchment into the bottom and sides of the dish, then lightly butter the parchment.

In a food processor, combine the graham crackers, sugar, and salt and process to form fine crumbs. Drizzle the melted butter over the graham cracker crumbs and process until combined. Dump the crumbs into the prepared dish and press them evenly over the bottom and slightly up the sides. Bake until the crust dries out slightly and starts to brown lightly, about 10 minutes. Let cool slightly while you make the filling.

In a bowl, using a whisk, beat together the eggs and yolks, sugar, salt, and lime zest. Beat in the lime juice, then the sour cream, and finally the flour. Carefully pour into the baked crust.

Bake until the filling is just set, about 13 minutes. Let cool completely in the dish on a wire rack, then refrigerate until cold. Use the parchment to lift the bars out of the dish, then cut into bars. Dust with confectioners' sugar or serve with dollops of whipped cream.

BAKER'S NOTE

Don't overbake the bars, or the texture will be too rubbery and the filling will crack. Take them out of the oven when the custard still jiggles a bit, kind of like Jell-O.

CHAPTER FOUR
CAKES & CUPCAKES

DEVIL'S FOOD
LAYER CAKE

*Is there anything more soul-satisfying
than a thick wedge of chocolate cake?
And this is a particularly good one—sturdy
yet tender and moist and perfect for
layering. It's a sure way to bring a smile
to anyone's face. Serve with a tall glass
of ice-cold milk for a hit of nostalgia.*

for the batter

¾ cup (2½ oz/75 g)
natural cocoa powder

⅔ cup (5 fl oz/160 ml)
boiling water

1 cup (8 fl oz/250 ml)
buttermilk

1¾ cups (9 oz/280 g)
all-purpose flour

1½ tsp baking soda

½ tsp kosher salt

¾ cup (6 oz/185 g)
unsalted butter, at
room temperature

1 cup (8 oz/250 g)
granulated sugar

½ cup (3½ oz/105 g)
firmly packed light
brown sugar

3 large eggs

2 tsp pure vanilla
extract

Vanilla Meringue
Buttercream (page 213),
or your favorite flavor,
such as espresso or
caramel

makes one 9-inch (23-cm)
double-layer cake

BAKER'S NOTE

If you want to make this even more elaborate,
slice the cakes into 2 layers (for a total
of 4 layers), then spread Chocolate Meringue
Buttercream (page 213) and fresh raspberries
between the layers. Coat with a double recipe
of Chocolate Ganache (page 132).

Position a rack in the middle of the oven and preheat to 350°F (180°C). Butter two 9-by-2-inch (23-by-5-cm) round cake pans and line the bottoms with parchment paper. Butter the paper and dust the pan with flour.

In a bowl, whisk the cocoa powder into the boiling water. Let cool to lukewarm, then whisk in the buttermilk. In another bowl, sift together the flour, baking soda, and salt.

In the bowl of a mixer fitted with the paddle attachment, beat the butter and sugars on medium speed until combined. Add the eggs one at a time, beating well after each addition. Add the vanilla along with the final egg. Reduce the speed to low and add the dry ingredients in 3 additions alternately with the cocoa-buttermilk mixture in 2 additions, starting and ending with the dry ingredients. Beat just until combined.

Divide the batter between the prepared pans. Bake until the cakes are puffed and slightly springy to the touch, and a toothpick inserted into the centers comes out clean, 22–25 minutes. Let the cakes cool in the pans for about 15 minutes, then invert onto wire racks to cool completely.

To frost the cake, place one layer, bottom side up, on a flat serving plate. Peel off the paper. Using a frosting spatula, spread evenly with about a third of the buttercream. Invert the other layer, bottom side up, onto the frosted layer and peel off the paper. Spread a very thin layer of the buttercream on the top and sides of the cake (this is your crumb coat, and will ensure that you have a pretty cake free of chocolate crumbs). Refrigerate the cake for about 30 minutes, then frost with the remaining buttercream. You can leave the cake out for a few hours before serving as long as it's not a super hot day; otherwise, refrigerate the cake until about an hour before serving. Let it come to room temperature before cutting into big, fat wedges.

COCONUT CUPCAKES
WITH LEMON CURD

These cupcakes are a whole lot of fun. Slathered with meringue frosting and topped with toasted coconut, they are fluffy balls of sweetness. Inside you'll find a surprise lemon filling that balances out the flavor of the tender coconut cake.

1¾ cups (7 oz/220 g) cake flour

2 tsp baking powder

¼ tsp kosher salt

¾ cup (6 oz/185 g) unsalted butter, at room temperature

1 cup (8 oz/250 g) sugar

3 large eggs

1 tsp pure vanilla extract

1 cup (4 oz/125 g) sweetened shredded coconut, plus 1 cup, lightly toasted (see Note) for garnish

¾ cup (6 fl oz/180 ml) buttermilk

Lemon Curd (page 215)

7-Minute Frosting (page 214) or Vanilla Meringue Buttercream (page 213)

makes 12 cupcakes

Position a rack in the middle of the oven and preheat to 350°F (180°C). Line 12 standard muffin cups with paper liners, or grease with butter and dust with flour.

In a bowl, sift together the flour, baking powder, and salt. In the bowl of a mixer fitted with the paddle attachment, beat the butter and sugar on medium-high speed until light, 2–3 minutes. Add the eggs one at a time, beating after each addition. Add the vanilla and beat until well combined. Beat in the 1 cup coconut. Add half of the flour mixture and beat on low speed until combined. Continuing to beat on low speed, add the buttermilk and then the remaining flour mixture.

Divide the batter among the prepared muffin cups, filling them about three-fourths full. Bake until lightly golden and a toothpick inserted into the center of a cupcake comes out clean, about 18 minutes. Let cool completely in the pan on a wire rack for 5 minutes. Transfer the cupcakes to the rack and let cool completely, about 1 hour.

Using a paring knife, create a hollow about 1½ inches (4 cm) in diameter and 1 inch (2.5 cm) deep in the center of each cupcake. Fill each hollow with a spoonful of the lemon curd.

Spread the filled cupcakes with a thick layer of the frosting (or pipe it on with a piping bag). Sprinkle with the remaining 1 cup toasted coconut. The filled and frosted cupcakes can be refrigerated in an airtight container for up to 4 days; bring to room temperature before serving.

BAKER'S NOTE

To toast coconut, spread it in an even layer on a baking sheet and bake at 325°F (165°C), stirring occasionally, until lightly golden, 5–10 minutes.

TROPICAL CARROT CAKE

Shredded carrots, toasted coconut, and juicy pineapple ensure that this spiced carrot cake stays ultramoist and extratasty. I leave out the toasted walnuts and raisins of the classic version, but feel free to add ¼ cup (1½ oz/45 g) of each.

2 cups (10 oz/315 g) all-purpose flour

1½ tsp baking soda

1 tsp kosher salt

1 tsp ground cinnamon

3 large eggs

1½ cups (12 oz/375 g) granulated sugar

1 cup (8 fl oz/250 ml) canola oil

1 tsp pure vanilla extract

4 large carrots, peeled and shredded (about 3 cups/8 oz/260 g)

1 can (6 oz/185 g) crushed pineapple, drained

1 cup (3 oz/90 g) sweetened shredded coconut, lightly toasted (page 15)

for the cream cheese frosting

¾ lb (375 g) cream cheese, at room temperature

6 tbsp (3 oz/90 g) unsalted butter, at room temperature

2 tsp pure vanilla extract

1½ cups (6 oz/185 g) confectioners' sugar, sifted

makes one 9-by-13-inch (23-by-33-cm) cake

Position a rack in the middle of the oven and preheat to 350°F (180°C). Butter and flour a 9-by-13-by-2-inch (23-by-33-by-5-cm) baking pan.

In a bowl, sift together the flour, baking soda, salt, and cinnamon to combine. In a large bowl, whisk together the eggs, granulated sugar, oil, and vanilla. Stir in the carrots, pineapple, and coconut. Stir in the dry ingredients just until incorporated. Spread the batter in the prepared pan.

Bake until a toothpick inserted into the center of the cake comes out clean, about 30 minutes. Let cool in the pan on a wire rack for about 15 minutes, then invert the cake onto the rack. Let the cake cool completely. Cover the cake with a slightly damp kitchen towel so that the surface does not dry out as the cake cools.

To make the frosting, in a bowl, using a mixer on medium-high speed, beat the cream cheese, butter, and vanilla until smooth, light, and fluffy, about 2 minutes. Gradually beat in the confectioners' sugar until thoroughly combined. If the frosting is too soft, refrigerate it until it is spreadable, about 15 minutes.

Transfer the cooled cake to a serving platter. Using an icing spatula, cover with a thick layer of frosting. Serve immediately, or store in an airtight container at room temperature for up to 3 days.

BAKER'S NOTE

While I prefer my carrot cake in one layer, old-school style, it's easy to turn this version into a layer cake for a more celebratory presentation. Divide the batter between two 9-inch (23-cm) cake pans and bake. Frost with the cream cheese frosting as you would a layer cake.

APPLE-WHISKY CAKE

Chock-full of apple chunks and spiked with a healthy glug of whisky, this simple-to-prepare, moist cake is seriously good. You can dress it up or down. Take squares in your lunch box for an afternoon treat, or serve slices with a scoop of ice cream after an autumn-inspired dinner.

---

4 baking apples (see Note), peeled, cored, and diced

⅓ cup (3 fl oz/80 ml) whisky (preferably something sweet not peaty), bourbon, or brandy

1¾ cups (9 oz/280 g) all-purpose flour

1½ tsp baking soda

¼ tsp kosher salt

¾ tsp ground cinnamon

¼ tsp freshly grated nutmeg

2 large eggs

1½ cups (10½ oz/ 330 g) firmly packed dark brown sugar

½ cup (4 oz/125 g) granulated sugar

1 cup (8 oz/250 g) unsalted butter, melted and cooled

Whipped Cream (page 214) for serving

makes one 9-by-13-inch (23-by-33-cm) cake

Position a rack in the middle of the oven and preheat to 325°F (165°C). Butter a 9-by-13-inch (23-by-33-cm) baking pan. Line the bottom and sides of the pan with a large piece of parchment paper that extends beyond the 2 sides of the pan and butter the parchment.

In a bowl, toss together the apples and whisky. In another bowl, sift together the flour, baking soda, salt, cinnamon, and nutmeg. In the bowl of a mixer fitted with the paddle attachment, beat the eggs and sugars on medium-high speed until thick and fluffy, about 3 minutes. Add the butter and beat until incorporated. Add the dry ingredients and stir together on low speed. Stir in the apples and whisky. Scrape the batter into the prepared pan and spread evenly.

Bake until the cake is a deep golden brown and a toothpick inserted into the center comes out clean, about 40 minutes. Let cool slightly in the pan for about 15 minutes, then carefully remove the cake by lifting it up with the parchment. Let the cake cool slightly on a wire rack before cutting into slices. Serve with big dollops of whipped cream.

BAKER'S NOTE

I use tart apples that are tender yet hold their shape when baked. Good options include Pink Lady (my personal favorite), Rome Beauty, Cortland, and Gravenstein. Also, like all fruit, apples are best when they are in season, in the fall and winter.

TRIPLE-DECKER
BIRTHDAY CAKE

What's a birthday celebration without a towering, decadent cake? This one's a true classic: yellow butter cake with a thin layer of raspberry jam and gooey fudge frosting, all waiting to be spiked with candles and presented to the lucky person for whom you made it.

for the yellow butter cake

2¾ cups (11 oz/345 g) cake flour

3 tsp baking powder

½ tsp kosher salt

1 cup (8 oz/250 g) unsalted butter, at room temperature

1¾ cups (14 oz/440 g) granulated sugar

4 large eggs

2 large egg yolks

2 tsp pure vanilla extract

1 cup (8 oz/250 g) sour cream

for the fudge frosting

1 cup (8 oz/250 g) unsalted butter, at room temperature

2½ cups (10 oz/315 g) confectioners' sugar, sifted

2 tsp pure vanilla extract

½ lb (250 g) unsweetened chocolate, melted and cooled

⅔ cup (6½ oz/200 g) raspberry jam

makes one 9-inch (23-cm) triple-layer cake

BAKER'S NOTE

When frosting a layer cake, place each layer top side down, as the bottom will tend to have a flatter surface and be easier to frost. If your cake layer is a little bit lopsided, use a long bread knife to trim it slightly to make it more even.

Position a rack in the middle of the oven and preheat to 350°F (180°C). Butter the bottoms of three 9-by-2-inch (23-by-5-cm) round cake pans. Line with parchment paper. Lightly butter the parchment and sides of the pans and lightly dust with flour.

To make the cake, in a bowl, sift together the flour, baking powder, and salt. In the bowl of a mixer fitted with the paddle attachment, beat the butter and granulated sugar on medium-high speed until fluffy. Add the whole eggs and yolks one at a time, beating well after each addition. Beat in the vanilla. Beating on low speed, add half of the dry ingredients and beat until combined. Beat in the sour cream and then the remaining dry ingredients, beating until combined.

Divide the batter among the prepared pans. Bake until a toothpick inserted into the center of the cakes comes out clean, 15–20 minutes. Let the cake layers cool in the pans on wire racks for 15 minutes, then invert the cakes onto the racks, peel off the parchment, and let cool before frosting.

To make the frosting, in the bowl of a mixer fitted with the paddle attachment, beat the butter on medium-high speed until fluffy. Add the confectioners' sugar and beat until light and fluffy, about 2 minutes. Beat in the vanilla. Add the cooled chocolate and beat on low speed until incorporated, then increase the speed and beat until light and fluffy, about 2 minutes.

To frost the cake, place one layer, top side down, on a flat serving plate. With an icing spatula, spread the top with a thin layer of frosting. Spread half of the raspberry jam over the frosting. Top with a second cake layer and top with a thin layer of frosting and the remaining jam. Top with the third cake layer. Cover the top and sides of the cake with a thick layer of the remaining frosting. Serve right away, cut into fat wedges, or keep covered at room temperature until ready to serve.

RED VELVET CUPCAKES
WITH CREAM CHEESE FROSTING

A real southern classic, red velvet cake has just a hint of cocoa and a deep red crumb. True to tradition, these party-worthy cupcakes are topped with rich cream cheese frosting and are embellished with a sprinkle of toasted sugared pecans.

2 tbsp natural cocoa powder

⅓ cup (3 fl oz/80 ml) boiling water

1 cup (8 fl oz/250 ml) buttermilk

¾ cup (6 oz/185 g) unsalted butter, at room temperature

1½ cups (12 oz/375 g) granulated sugar

3 large eggs

1 tsp red gel food coloring

2 tsp pure vanilla extract

½ tsp kosher salt

2½ cups (12½ oz/ 390 g) all-purpose flour

1½ tsp baking soda

1 tsp white distilled vinegar

for the cream cheese frosting

½ lb (250 g) cream cheese, at room temperature

4 tbsp (2 oz/60 g) unsalted butter, at room temperature

2 tsp pure vanilla extract

1 cup (4 oz/125 g) confectioners' sugar, sifted

Glazed Pecans (page 215)

makes 18 cupcakes

Position a rack in the middle of the oven and preheat to 350°F (180°C). Line 18 standard muffin cups with paper liners or grease with butter and dust with flour.

In a bowl, whisk the cocoa into the boiling water. Let cool to lukewarm, then whisk in the buttermilk. In the bowl of a mixer fitted with the paddle attachment, beat the butter and granulated sugar on medium-high speed until combined. Add the eggs one at a time, beating well after each addition. Stir in the food coloring, vanilla, and salt. Reduce the speed to medium-low and add the flour in 3 additions alternately with the buttermilk mixture in 2 additions, starting and ending with the flour. Beat just until combined. In a small bowl, stir together the baking soda and vinegar, then quickly stir into the batter.

Divide the batter among the prepared muffin cups, filling them about three-fourths full. Bake until puffed and a toothpick inserted in the center comes out clean, about 18 minutes. Let cool slightly, then remove the cupcakes from the pan and cool completely on a wire rack.

Meanwhile, make the frosting: In the bowl of a mixer fitted with the paddle attachment, beat the cream cheese, butter, and vanilla on medium-high speed until smooth, light, and fluffy, about 2 minutes. Gradually beat in the confectioners' sugar until thoroughly combined. If the frosting is too soft, refrigerate it until it is spreadable, about 15 minutes.

Spread the cupcakes with the frosting and sprinkle with the glazed pecans. The frosted cupcakes can be refrigerated in an airtight container for up to 4 days; bring to room temperature before serving. Dig in!

BAKER'S NOTE

These cupcakes are more of a brownish red than a bright red. If you want to amp up the color, replace 1 tablespoon of the cocoa with flour and add an extra teaspoon of red food coloring. You can substitute natural red food color (made from beets and/or hibiscus) for the standard food dye, but the color won't be nearly as vibrant.

ELISABETH PRUEITT
AND **CHAD ROBERTSON**

TARTINE

SAN FRANCISCO, CALIFORNIA

This well-loved neighborhood bakery opened its doors in 2002, and has had a line out the door ever since. It is renowned for its rustic, elegant pastries and desserts, such as the much-sought-after morning buns and seasonal bread pudding, as well as its incomparable levain. Elisabeth gave me the inside scoop on Tartine and her love of baking.

HOW LONG HAVE YOU BEEN BAKING?

All my life. I can't remember a time when I didn't bake. I was born the year the first Easy Bake oven came out and my mom gave me one when I was three and a half. I can still remember exactly what the chocolate cake smelled and tasted like.

WHAT RESTAURANT OR BAKERY HAS CHANGED YOUR LIFE?

My time working at Montrachet in New York City opened my eyes to the possibility that I could make this work my life.

WHAT DO YOU LOVE ABOUT TARTINE?

I love that when the bakers get an idea to make something new they get really excited and make test after test, and they involve everyone in the kitchen to taste it and solicit all of their co-workers' opinions.

WHAT'S YOUR FAVORITE THING TO BAKE?

Galettes. I love making the dough, rolling the dough by hand, making fruit fillings, and folding the sides up. I love how the dough feels and that each one is different. I think they are some of the most beautiful pastries to make.

SWEET OR SAVORY?

Sweets that have a savory element: salty caramel, cheese with figs, candied kumquats with fromage blanc, sweet caramelized onions, fermented honey with game.

TARTINE
ALMOND-ORANGE POUND CAKE

Bursting with the sweet flavor of almond paste and tangy orange zest and speckled with poppy seeds, this exceedingly moist pound cake is then gilded with a sugary citrus glaze. Inspired by a recipe from Flo Braker, it is the perfect accompaniment to a steaming cup of coffee or tea.

¾ cup (3 oz/90 g) cake flour, sifted

½ tsp baking powder

⅛ tsp kosher salt

5 large eggs

1 tsp pure vanilla extract

¾ cup (7 oz/220 g) almond paste, at room temperature

1 cup (8 oz/250 g) sugar

1 cup (8 oz/250 g) unsalted butter, at room temperature, cut into small chunks

2 tsp finely grated orange zest

1 tsp poppy seeds

for the glaze

¼ cup (2 fl oz/60 ml) fresh lemon juice

3 tbsp fresh orange juice

¾ cup (6 oz/185 g) sugar

makes 2 pound cakes

Position a rack in the lower third of the oven and preheat to 350°F (180°C). Butter and flour two 9-by-5-inch (23-by-13-cm) loaf pans.

Sift the flour, baking powder, and salt into a bowl. In another bowl, whisk together the eggs and vanilla just until combined. In the bowl of a stand mixer fitted with the paddle attachment, beat the almond paste on low speed until it breaks up, about 1 minute. Slowly add the sugar in a steady stream, beating until incorporated. (If you add the sugar too quickly, the paste won't break up as well.) Add the butter, a chunk at a time, beating just until combined. Raise the speed to medium and beat until the mixture is light in color and fluffy, 3–4 minutes. Continuing to beat on medium speed, drizzle the egg mixture into the butter mixture. Mix in the orange zest and poppy seeds. Add the dry ingredients in 2 additions, stirring after each until incorporated. Scrape the batter into the prepared pans.

Bake until the tops spring back when lightly touched and a toothpick inserted into the centers comes out clean, about 45 minutes. Let the cakes cool in the pans on a wire rack while you make the glaze.

To make the glaze, in a small bowl, stir together the lemon and orange juices and the sugar.

Place the wire rack holding the cakes over a sheet of waxed paper or foil. Invert the cakes onto the rack and place top side up. Brush the warm cakes with the glaze. Let the cakes cool completely on the rack, then cut into slices and serve.

CHOCOLATE MARSHMALLOW-CREAM CUPCAKES

A grown-up riff on Ding Dongs (one of my favorite treats to sneak as a kid), these chocolate cupcakes have a marshmallow-cream center and are coated with deep, dark ganache. If you want to make them look authentic, pipe a little swirl on top with thickened vanilla glaze (page 214).

Devil's Food Layer
Cake batter (page 118)

for the cream filling

¾ cup (3 oz/90 g)
confectioners' sugar

3 tbsp unsalted butter,
at room temperature

½ cup (4 oz/125 g)
purchased marshmallow
creme fluff

½ tsp pure vanilla
extract

1 tbsp heavy cream

for the ganache

1½ tbsp unsalted butter,
softened

6 oz (185 g) bittersweet
chocolate, finely
chopped

1½ tsp light corn syrup

6 tbsp (3 fl oz/90 ml)
heavy cream

makes 18 cupcakes

Position a rack in the middle of the oven and preheat to 350°F (180°C). Line 18 standard muffin cups with paper liners, or grease with butter and dust with flour.

Prepare the cake batter as directed and divide among the prepared muffin cups, filling them nearly full. Bake until the cupcakes are puffed and slightly springy to the touch, and a toothpick inserted into the center of a cupcake comes out clean, about 20 minutes. Let cool slightly, then remove the cupcakes from the pan and cool completely on wire racks.

To make the filling, in the bowl of a mixer, sift the sugar over the butter. Fit the mixer with the paddle attachment and beat on medium speed until lightened. Add the marshmallow fluff, vanilla, and cream and beat until light and fluffy.

Using a paring knife, create a hollow about 1½ inches (4 cm) in diameter and 1 inch (2.5 cm) deep in the center of each cupcake. Fill each hollow with a spoonful of the filling.

To make the ganache, in a heatproof bowl set over (but not touching) barely simmering water in a saucepan, melt the butter and chocolate with the corn syrup and cream, stirring constantly with a whisk until smooth. Remove from the heat and whisk until smooth. Let cool slightly.

Spread the filled cupcakes with the ganache. The filled and frosted cupcakes can be refrigerated in an airtight container for up to 4 days; bring to room temperature before serving.

BAKER'S NOTE

If you just want some good, old-fashioned chocolate cupcakes, omit the marshmallow cream filling and ganache topping. Bake the cupcakes as directed, then frost with Vanilla Meringue Buttercream (page 213) or Fudge Frosting (page 124).

BROWN BUTTER POUND CAKE
WITH FRESH FIG COMPOTE

Brown butter has an intoxicating aroma that is both buttery and nutty. It adds incredible richness to this vanilla pound cake. I've gilded the lily here by pairing the cake with a caramelized fig compote. You could also drizzle the whole thing with crème fraîche.

1 cup (8 oz/250 g) unsalted butter, at room temperature	**for the fig compote**
1¼ cups (10 oz/315 g) granulated sugar, plus 1 tbsp for sprinkling	About 12 fresh, plump figs, ideally Black Mission
4 large eggs	3 tbsp unsalted butter
1 large egg yolk	2 tbsp firmly packed dark brown sugar
2 tbsp whole milk	2 tbsp honey
¾ tsp kosher salt	Pinch of kosher salt
1½ tsp pure vanilla extract	1 tsp pure vanilla extract
1⅓ cups (5½ oz/170 g) cake flour	Vanilla ice cream for serving (optional)
½ tsp baking powder	makes 1 pound cake

BAKER'S NOTE

Figs have two fleeting seasons. The first is in early summer, and if you blink, it's gone. The second (and more robust) season is in late summer and early fall. The fruits in the second season tend to be sweeter and more full flavored. Look for figs that give when you squeeze them gently and also contain a few cracks. They'll always be sweeter.

In a small saucepan, melt the butter over medium heat. Reduce the heat to medium-low and simmer gently, swirling the pan often, until the butter is a toasty brown and smells nutty, about 4 minutes. Watch the butter carefully at the end, as it turns brown quickly. Scrape the butter into a bowl to stop the cooking and chill in the freezer just until it congeals but is not hard as a rock, 30–60 minutes.

Position a rack in the middle of the oven and preheat to 325°F (165°C). Butter and flour a 9-by-5-inch (23-by-13-cm) loaf pan.

In the bowl of a mixer fitted with the paddle attachment, beat the cold brown butter on medium-high speed until lightened in texture. Beating constantly, slowly drizzle in the 1¼ cups sugar. Continue to beat until light and fluffy. In another bowl, whisk together the whole eggs, egg yolk, milk, salt, and vanilla. Beating on medium-low speed, slowly drizzle the egg mixture into the butter mixture. Beat until combined and fluffy. Sift the flour and baking powder over the batter and gently fold in. Scrape the batter into the prepared pan. Sprinkle with the remaining 1 tablespoon sugar.

Bake until a toothpick inserted into the center of the cake comes out clean, 50–55 minutes. Let the cake cool in the pan on a wire rack for about 30 minutes. Turn the cake out onto the rack and let cool completely.

Meanwhile, make the compote: Trim the stems off the figs, then quarter them and set aside. In a cast-iron frying pan, warm the butter, sugar, honey, and salt over medium heat until syrupy and bubbling. Continue to cook for about 2 minutes, stirring constantly. Add the figs and vanilla and stir gently to coat. Set aside.

Serve thick slices of the cake topped with the fig compote and a scoop of ice cream, if desired.

DULCE DE LECHE CAKE

Someone brought a cake very similar to this to my birthday party one year, and it's been a favorite ever since, so I've re-created it here. The ultralight white cake, layers of decadent dulce de leche, and fluffy marshmallow-like frosting make this a melt-in-your-mouth dream.

for the vanilla chiffon cake

2 cups (8 oz/250 g) cake flour

2 tsp baking powder

1 cup (8 oz/250 g) sugar

⅓ cup (3 fl oz/80 ml) canola oil

2 tsp pure vanilla extract

4 large eggs, separated

½ tsp kosher salt

¼ tsp cream of tartar

for the filling

1 cup (8 fl oz/250 ml) *dulce de leche*

¼ cup (2 fl oz/60 ml) heavy cream

for the 7-minute frosting

3 large egg whites, at room temperature

¾ cup (6 oz/185 g) sugar

2 tbsp light corn syrup

⅛ tsp kosher salt

1 tsp pure vanilla extract

makes one 9-inch (23-cm) layer cake

BAKER'S NOTE

You can easily turn this into a lemon chiffon cake by swapping the *dulce de leche* filling with the same amount (or a bit more) of Lemon Curd (page 215). Add a few teaspoons of finely grated lemon zest to the cake batter for extra zing.

Position a rack in the middle of the oven and preheat to 350°F (180°C). Line two 9-by-2-inch (23-by-5-cm) round cake pans with parchment paper (do not butter the pan or parchment).

To make the vanilla chiffon cake, in a bowl, sift together the flour and baking powder. Whisk in half of the sugar. In a large bowl, whisk together the oil, vanilla, egg yolks, and ⅓ cup (3 fl oz/80 ml) plus 2 tablespoons water. In a third bowl, using a mixer fitted with the whip attachment, beat the egg whites, salt, and cream of tartar. When the egg whites get frothy, slowly add the remaining sugar, beating just until stiff peaks form. Whisk the dry ingredients into the oil mixture, then fold the egg whites into the batter. Divide the batter evenly between the prepared pans. Bake until a toothpick inserted into the centers comes out clean, 15–18 minutes. Let cool in the pans on wire racks for 15 minutes. Run a thin knife around the edges of the cake pans to loosen the cakes, then invert the cakes onto the racks, peel off the parchment, and let cool before filling and frosting.

To make the filling, in a bowl, beat together the *dulce de leche* and cream with a whisk until smooth.

Using a long serrated knife, cut each cake layer in half horizontally to create 4 thin layers total. Place one layer cut side down on a flat serving plate. Spread with a third of the filling (about ⅓ cup/ 3 fl oz/80 ml). Top with a second layer and spread with half of the remaining filling. Then top with a third layer and spread with the rest of the filling. Top with the fourth layer.

To make the frosting, in a heatproof bowl, whisk together the egg whites, sugar, corn syrup, salt, and ⅓ cup (3 fl oz/80 ml) water. Set the bowl over (but not touching) barely simmering water in a saucepan. Using a hand mixer, beat on medium-high speed to stiff peaks, about 5 minutes. Remove the bowl from over the water and continue to beat until the mixture cools, about 2 minutes. Add in the vanilla and beat until blended. Cover the top and sides of the cake with a nice thick layer of the fluffy frosting. Serve right away.

SUMMER FRUIT TRIFLE

When life gives you a bounty of juicy summer fruit—whether berries or peaches or cherries—prepare a trifle. Layers of light-as-air chiffon cake, whipped cream, vanilla custard, and loads of fresh fruit make up this gorgeous dessert that is perfect for a summer party.

for the vanilla custard

1 cup (8 fl oz/250 ml) heavy cream

2½ cups (20 fl oz/ 625 ml) whole milk

1 vanilla bean

6 large egg yolks

½ cup (4 oz/125 g) sugar

Pinch of kosher salt

3 tbsp cornstarch, mixed with 2 tbsp water

4–6 cups (1½–2¼ lb/ 750 g–1.1 kg) diced mixed summer fruit, such as raspberries, blackberries, strawberries, peaches, nectarines, apricots, or cherries

¼–½ cup (2–4 oz/ 60–125 g) sugar, depending on the sweetness of the fruit

1 layer Vanilla Chiffon Cake (page 134) or your favorite 9-inch (23-cm) light-textured vanilla cake

⅓–½ cup (3–4 fl oz/ 80–125 ml) sweet sherry

Whipped Cream (page 214) for serving

makes about 10 servings

To make the custard, in a medium saucepan, warm the cream and milk over low heat. Split the vanilla bean and scrape out the seeds with the back of a paring knife. Add the bean and seeds to the warm cream mixture. In another bowl, whisk together the egg yolks, sugar, and salt, then stir in the cornstarch mixture. Slowly pour about half of the warm cream mixture into the yolk mixture, whisking constantly. Pour the yolk mixture into the saucepan and raise the heat to medium-low. Cook, stirring constantly, until the custard is thickened, about 4 minutes. Pour through a medium-mesh sieve into a bowl, press a piece of plastic wrap on the surface of the custard, and let cool completely.

To assemble the trifle, in a bowl, toss the fruit with some sugar and set aside for about 20 minutes to macerate. Have ready a trifle bowl or a 3-qt (3-l) glass bowl measuring about 8 inches (20 cm) high and 8 inches (20 cm) in diameter. Cut the cake crosswise into thick slices (or you can cut it into chunks).

Line the bottom of the bowl with the cake slices, using about half of the slices. Sprinkle the cake with half of the sherry, then top with half of the fruit and half of the custard. Top with the remaining cake slices, sherry, fruit, and custard. Cover with plastic wrap and refrigerate for at least 2 hours.

Top the trifle with whipped cream before serving (you can also top with the whipped cream and refrigerate for an hour before serving). Use a big spoon to dig deep down into the trifle to make sure you get every delectable layer.

BAKER'S NOTE

For a special meal, make sweet little individual trifles by layering the ingredients in 6–10 glass serving cups or bowls.

WINTER PEAR TRIFLE

for the poached pears

1 cup (8 oz/250 g) sugar

6 ripe but firm pears, preferably Bosc, peeled, quartered, and cored

Peel from 1 orange, removed in strips with a vegetable peeler

½ vanilla bean

for the mascarpone cream

1 cup (8 oz/250 g) mascarpone cheese

3 tbsp sugar

1 tsp pure vanilla extract

Pinch of kosher salt

1½ cups (12 fl oz/ 375 ml) heavy cream

¼ cup (2 fl oz/60 ml) sweet marsala or sweet sherry

1 layer Devil's Food Cake (page 118) or your favorite 9-inch (23-cm) light-textured chocolate cake

⅓ cup (1½ oz/45 g) sliced almonds, toasted (page 15)

makes about 10 servings

To poach the pears, cut a circle of parchment that will fit in a large saucepan. Cut a small circle in the middle of the parchment. In the pan, bring 4 cups (32 fl oz/1 l) water and the sugar to a boil over high heat. Reduce the heat to medium, and add the pears and orange peel. Split the vanilla bean and scrape out the seeds with the back of a paring knife; add the pod and seeds to the saucepan. Lay the parchment in the saucepan to help submerge the pears. Adjust the heat so that the liquid simmers gently and poach the pears until tender, 15–20 minutes. Let cool in the poaching liquid.

To make the mascarpone cream, in the bowl of a mixer fitted with the whip attachment, beat the mascarpone, sugar, vanilla, and salt on medium speed just until combined. Add the cream and beat just to stiff peaks. Be careful that you don't overbeat the cream.

To assemble the trifle, in a small bowl, stir together the marsala and ¼ cup (2 fl oz/60 ml) of the pear poaching liquid. Cut the pears

into thick slices, place in a bowl, and toss with about ¼ cup of the poaching liquid (you can slice up some of the orange peel used in poaching and add that to the pears as well, if you like). Have ready a trifle bowl or a 3-qt (3-l) glass bowl measuring about 8 inches (20 cm) high and 8 inches (20 cm) in diameter. Cut the cake crosswise into thick slices.

Line the bottom of the bowl with half of the cake slices. Sprinkle with half of the marsala mixture. Top with half of the pear slices, including half of the juice, then spread with half the mascarpone cream. Top with the remaining cake slices, marsala mixture, and pear slices and juice. Spread with the remaining mascarpone cream. Cover with plastic wrap and refrigerate for at least 2 hours.

Sprinkle with the toasted almonds just before serving. Use a big spoon to dig deep down into the trifle to make sure you get a good helping of every layer.

While I usually think of trifle as a summertime treat, it's also a great choice with the rich, deep flavors of winter: chocolate cake, vanilla-poached pears, and decadent whipped mascarpone. It is a yummy addition to any holiday dinner party.

BAKER'S NOTE

Make sure to use plenty of juice from the pears to keep the trifle nice and moist. You can also use the vanilla custard from the Summer Fruit Trifle (page 137) and Whipped Cream (page 214) instead of the mascarpone cream.

LA TARTINE GOURMANDE
NUTTY RASPBERRY FINANCIERS

These sweet little gluten-free mini cakes are a French classic. They are the perfect afternoon snack served alongside a hot cup of tea. Almond meal, hazelnut flour, and amaranth flour can be found in most specialty or upscale markets.

½ cup (2 oz/60 g) almond meal

⅓ cup (1 oz/30 g) hazelnut flour

¼ cup (1 oz/30 g) amaranth flour or white rice flour

½ cup (4 oz/125 g) granulated sugar

¼ tsp kosher salt

1 vanilla bean

7 tbsp (3½ oz/105 g) unsalted butter

4 large egg whites

24 raspberries

Confectioners' sugar for serving

makes 8 financiers

BÉATRICE PELTRE
WWW.LATARTINEGOURMANDE.COM

Originally from France, and now living stateside, Béa always knew that she'd ultimately have a career in food. After teaching French abroad, she eventually followed her true passion and become a self-taught chef, food stylist, and photographer. La Tartine Gourmande brings to life her inspirations: a French upbringing, the fresh produce at the farmers' market, cooking for family and friends, and travel. Her award-winning blog offers recipes that, according to Béa, "make everyday food a beautiful and delicious experience."

Position a rack in the middle of the oven and preheat to 350°F (180°C). Line 8 standard muffin cups with paper liners or grease with butter. Line a baking sheet with parchment paper. Spread the almond meal and hazelnut flour on the prepared sheet and bake until fragrant, about 5 minutes. Let cool.

In a bowl, using a whisk, combine the toasted almond meal and hazelnut flour, amaranth flour, granulated sugar, and salt. Split the vanilla bean and scrape out the seeds with the back of a paring knife. In a small saucepan, combine the vanilla bean and seeds with the butter. Cook over medium heat until the butter melts, starts to brown lightly, and has a nutty aroma. Let cool for 3–4 minutes.

Beat the egg whites into the dry ingredients. Add the melted butter mixture in 3 additions, mixing well after each.

Divide the batter between the muffin cups and top with the raspberries, pressing them gently into the batter. Bake until the financiers are lightly golden brown, 18–20 minutes. Remove from the pan and let cool on a wire rack. Dust with confectioners' sugar before serving.

CHOCOLATE-BOURBON BUNDT CAKE

Every year my husband and I host Burns Night—complete with plenty of poetry, food, and booze—in celebration of Scotland's beloved poet Robert Burns. This cake, rich with chocolate and tinged with sweet bourbon, has found its place at that gathering and is a hit every year.

1 cup (8 oz/250 g) unsalted butter

4 oz (125 g) bittersweet chocolate, finely chopped

½ cup (1½ oz/45 g) natural cocoa powder

2 cups (10 oz/315 g) all-purpose flour

1 tsp baking soda

½ tsp kosher salt

3 large eggs

2 cups (1 lb/500 g) granulated sugar

1 cup (8 oz/250 g) sour cream

¾ cup (6 fl oz/180 ml) bourbon

2 tsp pure vanilla extract

for the dark chocolate glaze

¼ cup (2 fl oz/60 ml) heavy cream

4 oz (125 g) bittersweet chocolate, chopped

2 tbsp light corn syrup

1 tsp pure vanilla extract

Vanilla ice cream or Whipped Cream (page 214) for serving

makes 1 Bundt cake

Position a rack in the middle of the oven and preheat to 350°F (180°C). Butter and flour a 10-cup (2½-qt/2.5-l) Bundt pan.

In a small saucepan, melt the butter and chocolate over low heat, stirring with a whisk. Add the cocoa powder and stir until smooth. Let cool to room temperature.

In a bowl, whisk together the flour, baking soda, and salt. In the bowl of a mixer fitted with the paddle attachment, beat together the eggs and sugar on medium speed until lightened. Stir in the sour cream, bourbon, vanilla, and cooled chocolate mixture on low speed. Stir in the dry ingredients just until combined. Scrape the batter into the prepared pan.

Bake until a toothpick inserted into the center of the cake comes out clean, 40–45 minutes. Let cool in the pan on a wire rack for about 15 minutes. Unmold the cake onto the rack and let cool completely.

Meanwhile, make the glaze. In a small saucepan, warm the cream over low heat. Add the chocolate and corn syrup and stir with a whisk until the chocolate is melted and the glaze is smooth. Let cool to room temperature, then stir in the vanilla. Place the wire rack over a sheet of parchment paper or foil and pour the glaze over the top of the cake, letting it run down the sides. Slide the cake onto a serving platter. Serve thick slices with ice cream or whipped cream.

BAKER'S NOTE

Bundt cake pans can be rather elaborate, so be sure to grease all the nooks and crannies well, even if the pan has a nonstick surface. If the cake needs some help coming out of the pan, use a thin rubber spatula—rather than anything metal—to help ease it out.

PLUM
UPSIDE-DOWN CAKE

I love the drama of an upside-down cake, which emerges from the oven looking rather plain and boring, and then, once flipped out of the pan, turns into a bejeweled attraction, oozing with caramelized brown sugar and tender fruit. This version makes use of summer's juicy, sweet plums.

3 tbsp unsalted butter plus ½ cup (4 oz/125 g), at room temperature

¾ cup (6 oz/185 g) firmly packed light brown sugar

5 or 6 ripe but firm plums (about 1½ lb/750 g), such as Santa Rosa, halved, pitted, and quartered

1⅓ cups (5½ oz/170 g) cake flour

1½ tsp baking powder

¼ tsp kosher salt

¾ cup (6 oz/185 g) granulated sugar

2 large eggs

1 tsp pure vanilla extract

⅔ cup (5 fl oz/160 ml) buttermilk

Vanilla ice cream for serving

makes one 10-inch (25-cm) cake

In a 10-inch (25-cm) cast-iron pan, melt the 3 tablespoons butter over medium heat. Add the brown sugar and cook, stirring, until the sugar melts and bubbles, about 4 minutes. Let cool slightly. Carefully arrange the plum quarters in the pan in concentric circles.

Position a rack in the middle of the oven and preheat to 375°F (190°C).

In a bowl, sift together the flour, baking powder, and salt. In the bowl of a mixer fitted with the paddle attachment, beat the ½ cup butter and the granulated sugar on medium-high speed until light, 2–3 minutes. Add the eggs one at a time, beating well after each addition. Beat in the vanilla. On low speed, stir in half of the flour mixture, then the buttermilk, and the remaining flour mixture, beating just until combined.

Dollop the batter over the fruit and smooth it as evenly as you can. Bake until a toothpick inserted into the center of the cake comes out clean, about 40 minutes. Let cool in the pan on a wire rack for about 15 minutes.

Place a serving plate over the pan. Wearing oven mitts, carefully invert the plate and pan and unmold the cake. Serve the cake right away with big scoops of vanilla ice cream.

BAKER'S NOTE

Inverting an upside-down cake might seem intimidating, but it doesn't have to be. Wear oven mitts on both hands to protect them from the heat of the pan and the caramelized sugar. Use a flat serving plate that fits completely over the pan. Set the plate over the pan, place one hand on the plate and one on the bottom of the pan, and then quickly flip the two together. Lift off the pan. If bits of fruit are still stuck to the pan bottom, scrape them off and fill in any holes in the cake. Voila!

STICKY TOFFEE PUDDING

This just might be my favorite dessert in the book. It's a tender cake, of British origin, studded with honey-sweet dates and doused in a buttery toffee sauce. It is exquisitely rich and decidedly crave-worthy. To make it look even more gorgeous, add a dollop of whipped cream and a sliver of date.

½ cup (3 oz/90 g) pitted and finely chopped dates

¾ tsp baking soda

¾ cup (6 fl oz/180 ml) boiling water

4 tbsp (2 oz/60 g) unsalted butter, softened

¾ cup (6 oz/185 g) firmly packed dark brown sugar

2 large eggs

2 tsp pure vanilla extract

1 cup (5 oz/155 g) all-purpose flour

1¼ tsp baking powder

½ tsp kosher salt

for the toffee sauce

4 tbsp (2 oz/60 g) unsalted butter

¾ cup (6 oz/185 g) firmly packed dark brown sugar

¾ cup (6 fl oz/180 ml) heavy cream

2 tsp pure vanilla extract

Pinch of kosher salt

makes 8 servings

Position a rack in the middle of the oven and preheat to 350°F (180°C). Butter eight ½-cup (4–fl oz/125-ml) custard cups. Dust with flour and place on a baking sheet.

In a small bowl, combine the dates and baking soda with the boiling water. Let stand until cool, about 10 minutes. In the bowl of a mixer fitted with the paddle attachment, beat the butter and sugar on medium speed until lightened. Add the eggs one at a time, beating well after each addition. Beat in the vanilla. Add the flour, baking powder, and salt, and stir to combine. Add the date mixture and stir well. The batter will be thin. Fill the custard cups about two-thirds full.

Bake until the puddings are puffed and a toothpick inserted into the center comes out clean, about 20 minutes.

Meanwhile, make the toffee sauce: In a saucepan, melt the butter over medium heat. Add the brown sugar and cream, and stir with a whisk until the sauce gets sticky, about 5 minutes. Stir in the vanilla and salt.

To serve, unmold each warm pudding onto a plate and top with a big spoonful of the toffee sauce, letting it run all over the plate.

BAKER'S NOTE

Make a double batch of toffee sauce and reserve half to drizzle over any number of desserts, from scoops of vanilla ice cream to pound cake, and even over your morning buttermilk pancakes. It's that good!

MEYER LEMON PUDDING CAKE

As a big fan of citrus, especially lemons, I think nothing is as good as the incomparable Meyer lemon. This light and billowy "cake" showcases the fragrant fruit and is like a pudding and a soufflé in one.

6 tbsp (3 oz/90 g) unsalted butter, at room temperature

1¼ cups (10 oz/315 g) granulated sugar

1 heaping tbsp finely grated Meyer (or regular) lemon zest

5 large eggs, separated

½ cup (4 fl oz/125 ml) fresh Meyer (or regular) lemon juice

1½ cups (12 oz/375 g) sour cream

½ cup (2½ oz/75 g) all-purpose flour

½ tsp kosher salt

Boiling water as needed

Confectioners' sugar for dusting

Whipped Cream (page 214) for serving (optional)

makes about 8 servings

Position a rack in the middle of the oven and preheat to 350°F (180°C). Generously butter a 7½-by-12-inch (19-by-30-cm) or shallow 2-qt (2-l) baking dish with at least 2-inch (5-cm) sides. Have ready a roasting pan that will hold the dish (this will serve as your water bath).

In the bowl of a mixer fitted with the paddle attachment, beat the butter, granulated sugar, and lemon zest on medium-high speed until creamy. Add the egg yolks one at a time, beating well after each addition. Reduce the speed to low and add the lemon juice and sour cream and beat until smooth. Add the flour and stir until combined.

In another bowl, using clean beaters, beat the egg whites and salt on medium-high speed to medium-stiff peaks. Add about a fourth of the whites to the lemon batter and gently stir in to lighten the batter. Gently fold in the rest of the whites. Scrape the batter into the prepared dish. Place the dish in the roasting pan and carefully pour in boiling water to a depth of about 1 inch (2.5 cm).

Bake the cake until the top is golden brown and the center is just set, about 20 minutes. Remove from the water bath and let cool on a wire rack for about 15 minutes. Just before serving, dust the cake with confectioners' sugar. Serve big scoops of the cake topped with dollops of whipped cream, if desired.

BAKER'S NOTE

Meyer lemons used to be available only in Northern California, where I live, but they are slowly spreading across the country. Look for them during the winter months. If you can't find Meyers, just use regular lemons—the cake will be a bit more tart.

POLENTA–OLIVE OIL CAKE

Polenta and olive oil might not sound like natural ingredients for a cake, but they come together beautifully in this Italian-inspired treat, perfect for anyone who isn't a big fan of sweets. Serve wedges with halved, sugared red grapes, at the peak of their season in the autumn harvest months.

1⅓ cups (7 oz/220 g) all-purpose flour

2 tsp baking powder

½ tsp kosher salt

½ cup (2½ oz/75 g) polenta

3 large eggs, separated

1 cup (8 oz/250 g) granulated sugar

½ cup (4 fl oz/125 ml) aromatic white wine, such as Riesling or Gewürztraminer

½ cup (4 fl oz/125 ml) olive oil

1 tsp pure vanilla extract

Finely grated zest of 1 large lemon

Confectioners' sugar for sprinkling (optional)

makes one 9-inch (23-cm) cake

Position a rack in the middle of the oven and preheat to 350°F (180°). Butter a 9-inch (23-cm) springform pan. Line the bottom with parchment paper and butter the parchment.

In a large bowl, whisk together the flour, baking powder, salt, and polenta. In the bowl of a mixer fitted with the whip attachment, beat the egg yolks and granulated sugar on medium-high speed until thick and light, about 5 minutes. Add the wine, olive oil, vanilla, and lemon zest and beat to combine. Fold in the dry ingredients. In a separate bowl, using a clean whip attachment, beat the egg whites on medium-high speed to medium-stiff peaks. Fold the egg whites into the batter. Scrape the batter into the prepared pan.

Bake until the cake is golden brown and a toothpick inserted into the center comes out clean, about 40 minutes. Let the cake cool in the pan for about 15 minutes before removing the sides. Sprinkle with confectioners' sugar just before serving, if desired.

BAKER'S NOTE

Polenta, which is essentially just white or yellow cornmeal, is most often served as a savory Italian side dish. However, it also makes a delicious addition to a rustic cake. I tend to prefer a more finely ground polenta for cakes, but if you want a crunchier texture, choose a coarse grind.

CHAPTER FIVE

PIES & TARTS

RHUBARB TURNOVERS

When it comes to rhubarb, I'm a purest. Growing up, my mom often made rhubarb pie—never with strawberries—and that's how I like my pie filling to this day. And with its mouth-puckering tartness, rhubarb is particularly delicious in these flaky turnovers.

About 8 stalks rhubarb, cut into ½-inch (12-mm) pieces

About ⅔ cup (5 oz/155 g) granulated sugar

1 lb (500 g) frozen puff pastry, thawed

1 large egg, beaten with 1 tbsp water

Turbinado sugar for sprinkling

makes 8 turnovers

BAKER'S NOTE

Rhubarb, a vegetable (that's right, a vegetable, not a fruit), is plentiful in the springtime. Look for thin stalks without bruises or blemishes. Make sure you trim off all the leafy bits, as they are poisonous. The filling for these turnovers also makes a great compote or rustic preserves.

Combine the rhubarb and granulated sugar in a saucepan and simmer over medium heat, stirring occasionally, until the rhubarb releases its juices and becomes tender (but before it completely breaks down), about 3 minutes. Let cool completely.

Line 2 baking sheets with parchment paper. On a lightly floured work surface, roll out the puff pastry to a 24-by-12-inch (60-by-30-cm) rectangle. Cut out eight 6-inch (15-cm) squares. Place the squares on one of the prepared pans and refrigerate for 10 minutes.

Space 2 racks evenly in the middle of the oven and preheat to 400°F (200°C). Remove the chilled pastry squares from the refrigerator. Place a scant ¼ cup (1½ oz/45 g) of the rhubarb in the center of each square. Brush 2 connecting sides of the dough with a thin layer of egg wash and fold over to form a triangle. Crimp the edges with a fork. Arrange 4 turnovers on each prepared pan and refrigerate for about 10 minutes.

Lightly brush the turnovers with some more of the egg wash, sprinkle with turbinado sugar, and pierce the tops a few times with a fork. Bake until the turnovers are brown and puffy, 20–30 minutes, rotating the pans about halfway through. Let cool slightly, then serve while still warm.

CHERRY POTPIES

Potpies don't have to be savory. They make adorable desserts, and are a lot easier to put together than a large pie, as there's no need to line the bottom of a pan or worry about excess liquid, as when you slice into a pie. These cherry potpies are my favorite, especially if you can get your hands on a basket of fresh sour cherries.

Flaky Pie Dough for single crust (page 212)

2 large jars (24 oz/ 750 g each) sour cherries in juice or light syrup (you should have about 3 heaping cups of cherries without juice)

¼ cup (1½ oz/45 g) all-purpose flour

⅔ cup (5 oz/155 g) granulated sugar

1 large egg, well beaten with about 1 tsp water

Turbinado sugar for sprinkling (optional)

Vanilla ice cream for serving

makes 4 potpies

Prepare the flaky pie dough and chill as directed.

Drain the cherries, saving about ½ cup (4 fl oz/125 ml) of the juice. Put the cherries in a bowl. In a small bowl, mix the reserved juice with the flour and strain over the cherries. Stir in the granulated sugar. Divide the cherries and juice among four 1-cup (8–fl oz/ 250-ml) ramekins.

Position a rack in the middle of the oven and preheat to 375°F (190°C). Line a baking sheet with parchment paper.

On a lightly floured work surface, roll out the dough into a circle about ⅛ inch (3 mm) thick. Cut out 4 rounds of dough, each about ½ inch (12 mm) larger than the diameter of the ramekins. Place a dough round on top of each ramekin and press the edges down over the rim to secure. Cut a few vents in the dough. Brush with the egg wash and sprinkle with turbinado sugar, if desired.

Place the ramekins on the prepared pan and bake until the crust is golden and the cherry juices are bubbling, 35–40 minutes. Let cool for about 10 minutes. Serve the potpies topped with scoops of ice cream.

BAKER'S NOTE

Fresh sour cherries, such as the morello variety, can be hard to come by, and have a fleeting season. If you are lucky enough to find fresh ones, use them in these pies: Stem and pit the cherries, then simmer them in a saucepan over medium-low heat for a few minutes to release some of the juices, which you can then use as directed in the recipe.

UPSIDE-DOWN
PEACH COBBLER

Sweet, juicy, ripe peaches are the epitome of summer. Every year, during the peak of the season's heat, my family would pull out the hand-crank ice-cream maker and make peach ice cream. I like peaches any which way, whether eaten out of hand or bubbling away in an old-fashioned cobbler such as this one.

1 vanilla bean	1½ cups (7½ oz/235 g) all-purpose flour
½ cup (4 oz/125 g) unsalted butter	½ cup (4 oz/125 g) granulated sugar
6 or 7 large ripe but slightly firm peaches or nectarines, peeled, pitted, and cut into chunks (about 6 heaping cups/ 2¼ lb/1.1 kg)	2 tsp baking powder
	½ tsp baking soda
	½ tsp kosher salt
	1¼ cups (10 fl oz/ 310 ml) buttermilk
¼ cup (2 oz/60 g) firmly packed light brown sugar	Vanilla ice cream for serving
½ lemon	makes about 8 servings

Position a rack in the middle of the oven and preheat to 375°F (190°C). Have ready a 9-by-13-inch (23-by-33-cm) baking dish.

Split the vanilla bean and scrape out the seeds with the back of a paring knife. Add the pod and seeds to a frying pan along with the butter. Melt the butter over medium heat, swirling the pan occasionally, and cook until the butter starts to brown, about 3 minutes. Remove from the heat and discard the pod. Measure out ¼ cup (2 fl oz/60 ml) melted butter and set aside. Using a rubber spatula, scrape the rest of the melted butter and vanilla seeds into the baking dish, spreading it into an even layer.

In a bowl, toss the peaches with the brown sugar and a squeeze of lemon. In another bowl, whisk together the flour, granulated sugar, baking powder, baking soda, and salt. Add the buttermilk and the reserved ¼ cup melted butter and stir the ingredients just until they come together. Dollop the batter in the baking dish in as even a layer as you can (you might need to use your fingers; it's fine if the batter looks a little rough and patchy). Pour the peaches and their juices on top of the batter.

Bake until the fruit is tender and bubbling and the cobbler is cooked through, about 40 minutes. Serve warm with scoops of ice cream.

BAKER'S NOTE

As when making biscuits, make sure you don't overwork the batter here, or you'll end up with a chewy cobbler. Mix the ingredients just until they come together, and work quickly to spread the batter in the pan and get it in the oven.

APPLE-CINNAMON
HAND PIES

What baking book would be complete without some kind of apple pie? These old-fashioned mini pies are just the ticket. Stuffed with juicy apples tossed with brown sugar and cinnamon, then lightly coated in vanilla glaze, they are irresistible.

Flaky Pie Dough for double crust (page 212)

4 baking apples, peeled, cored, and cut into small chunks (scant 3 cups/12 oz/375 g)

Juice of ¼ lemon

⅓ cup (2½ oz/75 g) light brown sugar

¼ tsp ground cinnamon

1 tbsp all-purpose flour

1 large egg, beaten with 1 tsp milk

for the glaze (optional)

½ cup (2 oz/60 g) confectioners' sugar, sifted

¼ tsp pure vanilla extract

makes 8 hand pies

BAKER'S NOTE

It's important to always your pastry dough cold, so the butter doesn't melt into the dough and render the pie crust heavy and without flakes. If the dough gets too floppy or warm while you are rolling it out, slide it onto a baking sheet and place in the refrigerator for about 10 minutes to cool down.

Prepare the flaky pie dough and chill as directed.

Position a rack in the middle of the oven and preheat to 375°F (190°C). Line a rimmed baking sheet with parchment paper.

On a lightly floured work surface, roll out the dough into a large circle about ⅛ inch (3 mm) thick. Using an inverted bowl, cut out eight 6- or 7-inch (15- or 18-cm) circles of dough. You'll have to gather the scraps and reroll the dough a few times. Alternatively, you can divide the dough into 8 equal pieces and roll each piece into a circle. Place the circles on the prepared sheet and refrigerate for about 10 minutes.

In a bowl, toss together the apple chunks, lemon juice, brown sugar, cinnamon, and flour. Remove the dough circles from the refrigerator and place in an even layer on your work surface. Brush a thin layer of the egg wash around the border of half of each circle. Divide the filling among the dough circles, placing it in the middle of each circle. Fold the dough over the filling to make a half moon and press the edges with a fork to seal. Brush the tops with the remaining egg wash.

Bake until the hand pies are puffed and golden brown and oozing juice, 25–30 minutes. Set aside to cool on a wire rack.

To make the glaze, in a small bowl, whisk together the confectioners' sugar, vanilla, and 1 tablespoon water. Brush the glaze over the pies as soon as they come out of the oven while they are hot.

Serve the pies warm or at room temperature.

Matt Lewis and Renato Poliafito left their advertising careers behind to pursue their dream of opening a bakery. Since then, Baked has become a Brooklyn hot spot that takes the iconic American dessert a step further with inventions like Coca-Cola Bundt Cake, the Spicy Brownie, and Chocolate Marshmallows. It's all served up by an exceptionally friendly staff.

DO YOU EVER HAVE DESSERT FOR DINNER?

Matt: I have dessert for dinner almost twice a week. Sometimes, if I'm testing new recipes for the bakery, it's up to three times a week.

Renato: I always have to balance my sweet and savory. I always have dessert, even if it's just a bite of chocolate, but it has to be preceded by a savory meal.

WHAT INGREDIENT CAN YOU NOT LIVE WITHOUT?

Matt: Chocolate. If chocolate were to disappear, I'd be hard-pressed to get out of bed in the morning.

Renato: Chocolate and cheese. I agree with what Matt said, but I also wouldn't be able to get up in the morning if there weren't any cheese.

HOW OFTEN DO YOU LICK THE BOWL?

Matt: I rarely lick the bowl, but I do have a bad habit of spooning batter into my mouth in the good name of "taste testing."

Renato: So far, I've licked two bowls today.

HOW BIG IS YOUR SWEET TOOTH?

Matt: I'm not sure you can quantify it.

Renato: Oh gosh. It's pretty big.

BAKED
MISSISSIPPI MUD PIE

Don't be intimidated by this long recipe. It has many steps but you'll be rewarded with a masterpiece! To simplify the process, the pie can be made over two days: make the crust and cake on the first day, and the pudding and whipped cream on the day that you plan to serve it.

for the cookie crust

About 1 lb (500 g) chocolate sandwich cookies (about 40), such as Oreos, processed to very fine crumbs (about 3½ cups/ 10½ oz/330 g)

5 tbsp (2½ oz/75 g) unsalted butter, melted

Baked's Flourless Chocolate Cake batter (page 212)

for the pudding

¾ cup (6 oz/185 g) sugar

½ cup (1½ oz/45 g) natural cocoa powder

¼ cup (1 oz/30 g) cornstarch

¼ tsp kosher salt

4 large egg yolks

2½ cups (20 fl oz/ 625 ml) whole milk

3 tbsp unsalted butter

2 tsp pure vanilla extract

3 oz (90 g) dark chocolate, chopped

for the topping

1¼ cups (10 fl oz/ 310 ml) heavy cream

2 tbsp sugar

Chocolate shavings

makes 1 large pie

To make the crust, preheat the oven to 300°F (150°C). Lightly spray the bottom and sides of a 9-inch (23-cm) springform pan with nonstick cooking spray. Line the pan with parchment paper and lightly spray the parchment. Place the cookie crumbs in a bowl, add the melted butter, and stir until combined. Press the crumb mixture into the bottom and up the sides of the prepared pan. Chill in the freezer for about 10 minutes. Bake until the crust is dry to the touch, about 10 minutes. Let cool on a wire rack. Raise the oven temperature to 350°F (180°C).

Prepare the cake batter as directed, then pour the batter into the partially baked crust. Bake until the cake is set but still jiggles slightly, 38–42 minutes. Transfer to a wire rack and let cool completely. As it cools, the cake will deflate in the center and look sunken. Tightly wrap the cake and refrigerate for at least 3 hours or up to overnight.

To make the pudding, in a saucepan, whisk together the sugar, cocoa, cornstarch, and salt. Add the egg yolks and half of the milk and whisk until combined. Whisking constantly, slowly pour in the rest of the milk. Bring the mixture to a boil over medium heat, whisking constantly to prevent it from scorching. Cook for 30 seconds, then strain into a heatproof bowl. Add the butter, vanilla, and chocolate and whisk until combined. Continue to whisk to cool the mixture slightly. Let the pudding stand for 15 minutes. Cover with plastic wrap pressed directly onto the surface of the pudding to prevent a skin from forming. Refrigerate until chilled, 2–3 hours.

Stir the chilled pudding to loosen it, then pour on top of the cake, making sure to stay inside the crust. Spread the pudding in an even layer. Chill for at least 30 minutes. Meanwhile, whip the cream and 2 tablespoons sugar to medium peaks. Spread the whipped cream over the pudding. Sprinkle with chocolate shavings. Remove the sides of the pan, cut the pie into wedges, and serve. The pie can be kept, covered, in the refrigerator for up to 2 days.

APPLE FRANGIPANE TART

With its layers of flaky pastry, nutty-sweet almond frangipane, and thinly sliced apples, this tart makes a great last-minute dessert and is showstoppingly gorgeous. It's even more delicious served with lightly whipped crème fraîche.

1 sheet frozen puff pastry, about 10 by 14 inches (25 by 35 cm), thawed

for the frangipane

1½ cups (6 oz/185 g) sliced almonds, lightly toasted (page 15)

⅔ cup (5 oz/155 g) sugar

¼ tsp kosher salt

2 large eggs, lightly beaten

1 tsp pure vanilla extract

1 tsp pure almond extract

2 tbsp unsalted butter, melted

2 large baking apples, such as Pink Lady or Gravenstein

½ lemon

¼ cup (2½ oz/75 g) apricot jam for glazing (optional)

makes one 16-by-12-inch (40-by-30-cm) tart

BAKER'S NOTE

The ideal way to slice the apples is with a mandoline, so you can be sure the slices are ultrathin and even. If you don't have a mandoline, simply use a large, sharp knife to cut slices as thinly as possible.

Position a rack in the upper third of the oven and preheat to 425°F (220°C). Line a rimmed baking sheet with parchment paper.

On a lightly floured work surface, roll out the puff pastry into a 16-by-12-inch (40-by-30-cm) rectangle (it should just fit onto your baking sheet). Transfer to the prepared pan, fold over the edges to form a rim, and pinch the edges together. Refrigerate while you make the frangipane and prepare the apples.

To make the frangipane, in a food processor, combine the almonds, sugar, and salt and process until the almonds are finely ground. Add the eggs, vanilla and almond extracts, and melted butter and process until the mixture comes together.

Peel and core each apple (or you can leave them unpeeled, if you like). Slice them very thinly crosswise (this is easiest on a mandoline, but you can do it with a sharp knife). In a bowl, toss the apple slices with a squeeze of lemon juice.

Prick the chilled puff pastry all over with a fork. Bake until it looks dried out and very lightly browned, about 8 minutes. Remove from the oven and reduce the oven temperature to 350°F (180°C). Smear a thin, even layer of the frangipane on top of the pastry and then top evenly with the sliced apples. Bake until the tart is golden and the apples are tender-crisp, about 30 minutes. Transfer to a wire rack.

If you want to make the tart fancy, heat the jam in a saucepan over low heat until it liquefies. Pour through a fine-mesh sieve set over a small bowl. Using a pastry brush, gently brush the top of the tart with a thin coating of jam. Serve warm or at room temperature.

BLUEBERRY-ALMOND
CRISP

*When I want to make a quick,
no-fuss dessert, I almost always turn
to fruit crisp. I usually have all the
ingredients on hand—some seasonal
fruit and the components of crunchy
streusel. This crisp is quite juicy, perfect for
swirling with a scoop of melting ice cream.*

About 6 cups
(1½ lb/750 g) fresh
blueberries

3 tbsp granulated sugar
plus ¼ cup (2 oz/60 g)

1 tbsp all-purpose flour,
plus ¾ cup (4 oz/125 g)

½ cup (1½ oz/45 g)
rolled oats

⅓ cup (2½ oz/75 g)
firmly packed golden
brown sugar

¼ tsp kosher salt

½ cup (4 oz/125 g)
unsalted butter, at
room temperature,
cut into chunks

½ cup (2 oz/60 g) sliced
almonds, lightly toasted
(page 15)

Vanilla ice cream
for serving

makes about 8 servings

Position a rack in the middle of the oven and preheat to 375°F (190°C). Have ready a 9-inch (23-cm) square or 2½-quart (2.5-l) baking dish.

In the baking dish, toss together the blueberries, the 3 tablespoons granulated sugar, and the 1 tablespoon flour.

In a bowl, stir together the ¼ cup granulated sugar, the ¾ cup flour, the oats, brown sugar, and salt until well blended. Sprinkle the butter over the dry ingredients and use a pastry cutter or 2 kitchen knives to cut in the butter until the mixture looks like coarse crumbs. Stir in the almonds. Sprinkle the topping in an even layer over the blueberries.

Bake until the blueberries are tender when tested with a toothpick, the juices are bubbling, and the topping is golden brown, 35–40 minutes. Transfer to a wire rack and let cool for 10 minutes. Serve warm with scoops of ice cream.

BAKER'S NOTE

Crisps are incredibly versatile, so use whatever seasonal fruit you have on hand, from apples to nectarines. Be sure to remove the cores or pits, peel if needed, and cut the fruit into even-sized pieces. The baking time might change slightly. A crisp is done when the fruit is tender and bubbling and the topping is golden brown.

THE MIDNIGHT GALETTE

The first night I met my dear friend Andrew, we stayed up late drinking wine and preparing one of my favorite desserts, a galette: a fancy name for a simple, rustic, freestanding tart. We scavenged an array of fresh fruits, threw them all into the tart, and relished our creation at midnight, hence the name, which has forever stuck.

Flaky Pie Dough for double crust (page 212)

5–6 cups (25–30 oz/ 780–940 g) peeled, cored or pitted, and cut-up mixed seasonal fruit, such as peaches, berries, cherries, and apricots

Juice of ½ lemon

About ⅓ cup (3 oz/90 g) granulated sugar, depending on the sweetness of the fruit

2 tbsp all-purpose flour

1 large egg, beaten with 1 tsp water

Turbinado sugar for sprinkling

makes 1 large galette

Prepare the flaky pie dough and chill as directed.

Preheat the oven to 400°F (200°C). Line a rimmed baking sheet with parchment paper.

In a large bowl, toss the fruit with the lemon juice. Add ⅓ cup granulated sugar and the flour and toss to mix. Taste for sweetness and add a bit more sugar if needed.

On a lightly floured work surface, roll out the dough into a large oval about ⅛ inch (3 mm) thick. As you roll, continuously rotate the dough a quarter of a turn and sprinkle it with flour to keep it from sticking. It's also a good idea to flip the dough over. If the dough rips or tears, press it back together and roll over it. Gently roll up the dough onto the rolling pin. Starting at one end of the prepared baking sheet, unroll the dough so that it is centered on the sheet. It is fine if the dough is a bit larger than the sheet.

Dump the fruit filling into the center of the dough and spread evenly with your hands, leaving a 3-inch (7.5-cm) border of dough. Fold the edges of the dough up and over the filling, all the way around the filling, pleating the dough as you fold. Brush the rim with the egg wash and sprinkle with turbinado sugar.

Bake the galette until the fruit is tender, the juices are bubbling, and the crust is golden brown, 45–60 minutes. Transfer to a wire rack. Serve warm or at room temperature.

BAKER'S NOTE

When rolling out dough, always begin with a cold disk of dough and a large flat work surface that's been dusted with flour. Start from the center of the disk and roll toward—but not over—the edges. Lift and turn the dough, and occasionally flip it over, to make sure it doesn't stick to the surface and to help keep a more round shape.

NECTARINE LATTICE PIE

When I was growing up, we baked a lot of fruit pies—pies were among the first recipes I learned to master in the kitchen. I was always impressed with lattice-topped pies. Seemingly intricate, they are actually quite easy to put together. I like them best with a colorful fruit filling, such as nectarines, peaches, or cherries.

Flaky Pie Dough for double crust (page 212)

About 7 ripe nectarines, pitted and sliced

About ½ cup (4 oz/ 125 g) granulated sugar, depending on the sweetness of the fruit

½ lemon

¼ cup (1½ oz/45 g) all-purpose flour

1 large egg, beaten with 1 tbsp water

Turbinado sugar for sprinkling (optional)

makes one 9-inch (23-cm) pie

BAKER'S NOTE

I often simply lay the strips of dough on top of each other to create the lattice, but if you want to get fancy, lay five strips of dough on the pie filling. Fold back every other strip halfway, and lay down a strip perpendicular across the unfolded strips. Repeat to place five strips of dough evenly across the top, folding back the alternate strips each time.

Prepare the flaky pie dough and chill as directed.

Position a rack in the middle of the oven and preheat to 375°F (190°C).

In a bowl, toss the nectarine slices with ½ cup granulated sugar and a squeeze of lemon. Taste for sweetness and add a bit more sugar if needed. Set aside for about 20 minutes.

Divide the dough in half. On a lightly floured work surface, roll out one half into a circle about 13 inches (33 cm) in diameter and ⅛ inch (3 mm) thick. Line a deep 9-inch (23-cm) pie pan with the dough. Refrigerate while you roll out the remaining dough. Roll the dough to a rough circle about 11 inches (28 cm) in diameter. Using a 1-inch (2.5-cm) wide ruler as a guide, cut 10 strips of dough.

Sprinkle the flour over the nectarines and stir together. Pour the nectarines and juices into the lined pie pan. Lay 5 strips of dough evenly across the top, using the longest strips in the center and the shorter strips on the sides. Brush lightly with the egg wash. Lay the remaining 5 strips perpendicular to the other strips, spacing them evenly. You can also weave the strips together (see Note). Trim the ends of the strips, ideally so they extend ½ inch (12 mm) beyond the pan (don't worry if the dough isn't completely even). Tuck the dough under itself to create a rim. Use your fingers or a fork to make a decorative rim. Lightly brush the top of the pie with more of the egg wash and sprinkle with turbinado sugar, if desired.

Bake until the crust is golden brown and the fruit is bubbly and soft, 45–60 minutes, depending upon the ripeness of the fruit. Let cool for at least 1 hour before slicing.

ITSY-BITSY
LEMON MERINGUE PIES

Let's face it: making a lemon meringue pie is not an easy endeavor. But the rewards are great, especially if, like me, you are a major lemon fan. These little pies take some effort, but they are adorable, perfect for a party, and will impress your guests.

Flaky Pie Dough for single crust (page 212)	**⅓ cup (3 fl oz/80 ml) fresh lemon juice, strained**
for the filling	**2 tbsp unsalted butter**
¾ cup (6 oz/185 g) sugar	*for the meringue*
3 tbsp cornstarch	**4 large egg whites**
Pinch of kosher salt	**Pinch of cream of tartar**
Finely grated zest of 2 lemons	**Pinch of kosher salt**
4 large egg yolks, beaten	**½ cup (4 oz/125 g) sugar**
	makes about 3 dozen mini pies

BAKER'S NOTE

You can easily make this recipe into a 9-inch (23-cm) pie. Line the pan and prebake as directed on page 172 until golden, increasing the time by 5–10 minutes. Then follow the directions here to fill, top, and bake the pie, adding about 5 minutes for browning the meringue.

Prepare the flaky pie dough and chill as directed.

Lightly butter two 24-cup mini muffin pans. On a lightly floured work surface, roll out the dough quite thin, to ¹⁄₁₆–⅛ inch (2–3 mm) thick. Using a 2½-inch (6-cm) round cutter, cut out as many disks as you can. Gather the scraps, press together, reroll, and cut more disks. You should have around 40 disks total. Gently press each disk into a muffin cup to line it evenly. Chill in the refrigerator for at least 20 minutes.

Position a rack in the middle of the oven and preheat to 375°F (190°C). Fill any empty muffin cups with a little water. Prick the bottoms of the shells with a fork. Bake the shells until golden brown, about 13 minutes. Let cool for about 5 minutes, then remove the shells from the pans and place on a rimmed baking sheet.

Have ready all the ingredients for the filling and meringue before you get started. In a saucepan, whisk together the sugar, cornstarch, and salt. Whisk in 1 cup (8 fl oz/250 ml) water and the lemon zest and bring to a boil over medium-high heat, stirring constantly until the mixture starts to thicken. Place the yolks in a bowl, pour in a bit of the hot sugar mixture, and whisk together. Pour the yolks into the saucepan and whisk to combine. Bring to a simmer over medium-low heat, whisking constantly. Whisk in the lemon juice, then the butter. The mixture should be quite thick. Using a small spoon, fill the baked shells with the lemon filling. Place in the oven to stay warm while you make the meringue (you don't want to leave the shells in the oven longer than 5 minutes, so you will need to work quickly!).

To make the meringue, in the bowl of a mixer fitted with the whip attachment, beat the egg whites, cream of tartar, and salt on medium-high speed until frothy. Beating constantly, slowly sprinkle in the sugar. Beat until the meringue is thick and glossy (when you stop the beaters, the peaks should just barely curl at the ends).

Dollop the meringue on the pies, doing your best to spread it to the edges of the filling to seal the filling in the shells. You can also use a pastry bag and a medium tip to pipe the meringue onto the pies. Bake until the meringue is golden brown, 5–8 minutes. Let the pies cool completely before serving.

APRICOT-PISTACHIO TART

This alluring tart, with its fragrant pistachio crust and plump, tart apricot filling, makes me think of the warm, sunny Mediterranean. As with all fruit, apricots are best in their summer season, and hard to find out of season, so grab them when you see them at the market.

for the pistachio crust

½ cup (2 oz/60 g) unsalted, shelled pistachios, chopped, plus more for topping

¼ cup (2 oz/60 g) sugar

1 cup (5 oz/155 g) all-purpose flour

½ tsp kosher salt

8 tbsp (4 oz/125 g) cold unsalted butter, cut into chunks

1 large egg yolk

About 8 ripe but slightly firm apricots, pitted and sliced

Scant ½ cup (4 oz/125 g) sugar

¼ lemon

1 tbsp cornstarch, mixed with 1 tbsp cold water

1 cup (8 oz/250 g) crème fraîche

2 tbsp honey

makes one 9-inch (23-cm) tart

To make the crust, in a food processor, pulse the pistachios and sugar until finely ground. Add the flour and salt and pulse until combined. Add the butter and egg yolk and pulse until the dough is crumbly.

Scrape the dough into a 9-inch (23-cm) tart pan with a removable bottom. Scoop out ½ cup (3 oz/90 g) of the crumbly dough and set aside. Using the bottom of a glass, press the dough over the bottom and up the sides of the pan to create an even layer. Refrigerate for about 30 minutes.

Position a rack in the middle of the oven and preheat to 375°F (190°C).

In a large bowl, toss the apricots with the sugar, then squeeze the lemon over the apricots. Stir in the cornstarch mixture. Pour the apricot mixture, including the juices, into the lined tart pan. Sprinkle the reserved crumbly dough and the extra chopped pistachios over the top of the tart.

Bake until the tart is golden brown and bubbly, 45–50 minutes. Transfer to a wire rack and let cool completely. In a small bowl, beat the crème fraîche and honey until thick and fluffy. Serve wedges of the tart topped with dollops of the honey–crème fraîche.

BAKER'S NOTE

Crème fraîche is a French-style thickened cream similar to sour cream. If you want to use sour cream instead, use about half sour cream and half heavy cream, then whip into fluffy mounds as directed.

BANANA-RAMA
CHOCOLATE CREAM PIE

This multi-layered, heavenly cream pie might just be the best I've ever had. A gooey layer of dark chocolate ganache seals in the crisp pastry, and silky custard lovingly envelops sliced bananas. Fluffy whipped cream embellished with chocolate shavings tops it all off.

Flaky Pie Dough for single crust (page 212)

for the ganache
1 tbsp unsalted butter
3 oz (90 g) bittersweet chocolate, chopped
¼ cup (2 fl oz/60 ml) heavy cream

for the custard
½ cup (4 oz/125 g) sugar
¼ cup (1 oz/30 g) cornstarch
¼ tsp kosher salt

2 cups (16 fl oz/500 ml) whole milk
½ vanilla bean
4 large egg yolks
2 tbsp unsalted butter

2 large or 3 small ripe but firm bananas

Whipped Cream (page 214)

Chunk of bittersweet chocolate to make curls for garnish

makes one 9-inch (23-cm) pie

BAKER'S NOTE

To line a pie pan, carefully roll the dough around the rolling pin, position it over the pan, and unroll. Lift the edges and press the dough into the bottom and sides without stretching it. Trim the edge, leaving at least a ½-inch (12-mm) overhang, then roll the extra dough underneath itself to create a rim. Use a fork or your fingers to create a fluted edge.

Prepare the flaky pie dough and chill as directed. On a lightly floured work surface, roll out the dough into a circle about 13 inches (33 cm) in diameter and ⅛ inch (3 mm) thick. Line a deep 9-inch (23-cm) pie pan with the dough. Trim the edges so they extend about ½ inch (12 mm) beyond the pan. Tuck the dough under itself to create a rim. Use your fingers to make a decorative rim. Chill in the freezer for 20 minutes.

Position a rack in the middle of the oven and preheat to 400°F (200°C). Line the pie shell with foil and fill with pie weights or dried beans. Bake until the crust starts to look dry, about 15 minutes. Remove the foil and weights and bake until the crust is golden brown, 10–15 minutes. Let cool.

Meanwhile, make the ganache: In a saucepan, melt the butter and chocolate with the cream over low heat, stirring constantly just until smooth. Pour into a large bowl and let cool for 15–20 minutes. Whisk until smooth, then spread in the bottom of the crust in an even layer.

To make the custard, in a saucepan, whisk together the sugar, cornstarch, and salt. Slowly whisk in the milk. Split the vanilla bean and scrape out the seeds with the back of a paring knife. Add the pod and seeds to the milk mixture. Bring to a simmer over medium heat. In another bowl, whisk the egg yolks. Add a little of the warm milk mixture to the yolks, whisking constantly. Whisk the egg yolks back into the warm milk mixture. Cook over medium heat, stirring constantly, until the custard thickens, about 6 minutes. Continue to cook for about 1 minute longer. Remove from the heat and stir in the butter. Pour through a medium-mesh sieve into a bowl, then cover with plastic wrap, pressing it directly onto the surface of the custard to prevent a skin from forming. Let cool for 15 minutes. Do not let the custard cool completely.

Dollop half of the warm custard over the chocolate layer, spreading it evenly and doing your best not to disturb the chocolate. Peel and slice the bananas. Arrange them in an even layer on top of the custard. Dollop the remaining custard over the bananas and spread evenly, covering the bananas and sealing the custard to the pie shell. Cover with plastic wrap and refrigerate the pie until chilled, at least 3 hours.

Before serving, mound the whipped cream on top of the pie, then shave dark chocolate all over the top.

MAPLE
PUMPKIN PIE

To me, Thanksgiving dinner isn't right without a big slice of homemade pumpkin pie topped with a dollop of whipped cream. This is my favorite version: a creamy pumpkin custard spiced with cinnamon, nutmeg, and ginger and sweetened with the luscious flavors of brown sugar and maple syrup. Pass me another slice, please!

Flaky Pie Dough for single crust (page 212)

1 can (15 oz/470 g) pumpkin puree (about 1½ cups)

⅔ cup (5 oz/155 g) firmly packed light brown sugar

½ cup (5½ oz/170 g) maple syrup

¾ cup (6 fl oz/180 ml) whole milk

½ cup (4 fl oz/125 ml) heavy cream

2 large eggs, lightly beaten

2 tbsp all-purpose flour

1 tsp ground cinnamon

¼ tsp ground ginger

⅛ tsp freshly grated nutmeg

½ tsp kosher salt

Whipped Cream (page 214) for serving

makes one 9-inch (23-cm) pie

Prepare the flaky pie dough and chill as directed. On a lightly floured work surface, roll out the dough into a circle about 13 inches (33 cm) in diameter and ⅛ inch (3 mm) thick. Line a deep 9-inch (23-cm) pie pan with the dough. Trim the edges so they extend about ½ inch (12 mm) beyond the pan (don't worry if the dough isn't completely even). Tuck the dough under itself to create a rim. Use your fingers or a fork to make a decorative rim. Chill in the freezer for about 20 minutes.

Position a rack in the middle of the oven and preheat to 400°F (200°C). Line the pie shell with foil and fill with pie weights or dried beans. Bake until the crust starts to look dry, about 15 minutes. Remove the foil and weights and bake until the crust is just barely golden, about 5 minutes. Remove from the oven and reduce the oven temperature to 350°F (180°C).

In a large bowl, whisk together the pumpkin, brown sugar, and maple syrup. In another bowl, whisk together the milk, cream, and eggs. Whisk into the pumpkin mixture. Sift the flour, cinnamon, ginger, nutmeg, and salt over the pumpkin mixture and whisk to combine.

Place the pie pan on a baking sheet. Pour the filling into the shell. Bake until the filling is just set and still jiggles very slightly in the center when gently moved, 60–70 minutes. Let cool on a wire rack for at least 1 hour.

Serve wedges of the pie with big spoonfuls of whipped cream.

BAKER'S NOTE

Using canned pumpkin is not a sin. I always use it in pie, because the consistency stays the same and you don't have to worry about the level of sweetness or amount of water present in a pumpkin. You can, of course, make your own pumpkin puree: Start with a sugar pie or other small baking pumpkin. Peel and seed it, cut it into chunks, and roast it until tender at 375°F (190°C). Puree it until smooth in a food processor.

BUTTERMILK PIE
WITH RASPBERRIES

Buttermilk pie makes me think of my home state of Texas, where the pie is exceedingly popular. Lest you think it sounds strange, I encourage you to give it a chance, because this is a beautifully balanced custard with the tang of buttermilk and a hint of lemon zest and vanilla.

Flaky Pie Dough for single crust (page 212)

½ cup (4 oz/125 g) unsalted butter, at soft room temperature

1 cup (8 oz/250 g) granulated sugar

¼ cup (2 oz/60 g) firmly packed light brown sugar

3 large eggs, beaten

2 tbsp all-purpose flour

Pinch of kosher salt

1 cup (8 fl oz/250 ml) buttermilk

1½ tsp pure vanilla extract

½ tsp finely grated lemon zest

2 cups (8 oz/250 g) raspberries

Confectioners' sugar for sprinkling (optional)

makes one 9-inch (23-cm) pie

Prepare the flaky pie dough and chill as directed.

On a lightly floured work surface, roll out the dough into a circle about 13 inches (33 cm) in diameter and ⅛ inch (3 mm) thick. Line a 9-inch (23-cm) pie pan with the dough. Trim the edges so they extend about ½ inch (12 mm) beyond the pan (don't worry if the dough isn't completely even). Tuck the dough under itself to create a rim. Use your fingers or a fork to make a decorative rim. Refrigerate the pie shell for about 20 minutes.

Position a rack in the middle of the oven and preheat to 400°F (200°C). Line the pie shell with foil and fill with pie weights or dried beans. Bake until the dough starts to look dry, about 15 minutes. Remove the foil and weights and bake until the crust is very lightly golden, about 5 minutes. Remove from the oven and reduce the oven temperature to 350°F (180°C).

In the bowl of a mixer fitted with the paddle attachment, beat the butter and sugars on medium speed until lightened, about 3 minutes. Beat in the eggs. Stir in the flour, salt, buttermilk, vanilla, and lemon zest. Pour the filling into the shell. Bake until the top is golden brown and the custard has set, about 45 minutes. Let cool completely, then pile the raspberries on top before serving. Dust with confectioners' sugar, if you like.

BAKER'S NOTE

A handful of fresh raspberries makes the perfect counterpoint to the richness of the pie, but any tart-sweet fruit would be delicious. Try blackberry or rhubarb compote or sliced fresh strawberries and whipped cream.

TERESA ULRICH
PEARL BAKERY
PORTLAND, OREGON

Located in Portland's Pearl District, this formerly small artisanal bakery was one of the first businesses on its block. Today, the popular spot has grown with its vibrant neighborhood, but still holds on to its core values by taking pride in everything it does, from serving handcrafted breads, sandwiches, and pastries made with the finest ingredients available to taking an active role in the community and environment.

WHAT INGREDIENT CAN YOU NOT LIVE WITHOUT?
I couldn't bake much without flour, which would be the end of Pearl Bakery's delightful breads, cakes, and cookies. But chocolate courses through my veins; I'd be personally devastated without chocolate.

WHAT'S THE BEST PART OF BAKING BREAD?
The cozy toasty aroma of bread crust caramelizing while it's being baked is the best part about making bread! Bread has a long history and I enjoy the connection to this ancient heritage whenever I work with bread. Good bread comes from centuries of knowledge and a respect for the delicate chemistry involved. When mastered, it's a very satisfying feeling.

HOW MANY LOAVES OF BREAD DO YOU TURN OUT EVERY DAY?
We have a strong bread department hand-shaping 1000 loaves and 1500 rolls a day on average. We use 10,000 pounds of bread flour in one week.

SWEET OR SAVORY?
Sweet! But not too sweet...just enough sweetness to enhance flavor, but not overwhelm it.

WHAT'S THE BEST THING ABOUT YOUR CITY?
I'm proud of Portland's colorful range of handcrafted food and drink-focused businesses. It's a relaxed and creative city with very imaginative food.

PEARL BAKERY
BLUEBERRY-HUCKLEBERRY GRAND MARNIER TART

This luscious tart pays tribute to the huckleberries that grow abundantly in the Pacific Northwest. If you can't find fresh huckleberries where you live, substitute frozen ones or increase the amount of blueberries and toss them in huckleberry jam.

for the dough

½ cup (4 oz/125 g) unsalted butter, at room temperature

¼ cup (2 oz/60 g) sugar

⅛ tsp kosher salt

1 large egg, beaten

1¼ cups (6½ oz/200 g) all-purpose flour

⅛ tsp baking powder

2½ tsp fresh orange juice

¾ tsp pure vanilla extract

for the filling

3 tbsp huckleberry, blueberry, or seedless blackberry jam plus ½ cup (5 oz/155 g)

1 large egg

½ cup (4 oz/125 g) sugar

1½ tsp pure vanilla extract

½ cup (4 oz/125 g) crème fraîche

½ cup (4 fl oz/125 ml) whole milk

5 tbsp (3 fl oz/80 ml) heavy cream

1 tbsp Grand Marnier

¼ cup (1½ oz/45 g) plus 1 tbsp flour

1½ cups (6 oz/185 g) blueberries

½ cup (2 oz/60 g) huckleberries

makes one 9-inch (23-cm) tart

To make the dough, in the bowl of a mixer fitted with the paddle attachment, mix the butter, sugar, and salt on low speed just until blended. Continuing to mix on low speed, slowly add the egg. Add half of the flour and the baking powder, then the orange juice and vanilla, and the remaining flour, mixing each just until combined. Transfer the dough to a floured work surface and knead gently. Form into a disk, wrap with plastic wrap, and chill for 1 hour.

On a lightly floured surface, roll the dough into a circle about 12 inches (30 cm) in diameter and ⅛ inch (3 mm) thick. Drape the dough over the rolling pin and ease it into a 9-inch (23-cm) tart pan with a removable bottom. Trim the dough to about ½ inch (12 mm) above the edge of the pan and fold over, pressing the dough to raise it slightly above the rim. Prick the bottom with a fork, cover with plastic wrap, and freeze until thoroughly frozen, about 1 hour.

Preheat the oven to 350°F (180°C). Coat both sides of a large piece of foil with nonstick cooking spray, then wrap it tightly around the frozen tart shell. Fill with pie weights. Bake the crust until lightly golden brown, about 25 minutes. Set on a wire rack to cool for 20 minutes. Remove the foil and weights and let cool.

Spread the 3 tablespoons jam over the bottom of the crust. In a bowl, whisk together the egg, sugar, and vanilla. Whisk in the crème fraîche, milk, cream, and Grand Marnier. Sift the flour over the mixture and whisk well to blend. Let stand for 5 minutes. Skim any foam from the surface, stir, then pour the batter into the crust. Bake until the center is just set, about 20 minutes. Let cool completely on a wire rack.

In a bowl, toss the blueberries with about two-thirds of the remaining ½ cup jam until just coated. Gently spread evenly over the tart. Toss the huckleberries with the remaining jam and spread evenly over the blueberries, filling in the empty spaces. Cut into wedges and serve.

MINI CHOCOLATE PUDDING PIES

Rich, decadent, and intensely chocolatey, these mini pies are the ultimate chocolate lover's dream. If you don't have time to make the whole shebang, the pudding is perfect on its own. Spoon it into individual serving bowls while it's still warm, cover with plastic, and chill until ready to eat. Dollop each bowlful with whipped cream.

Flaky Pie Dough for double crust (page 212)

½ cup (4 oz/125 g) sugar

¼ cup (¾ oz/20 g) natural cocoa powder

3 tbsp cornstarch

¼ tsp kosher salt

¼ cup (2 fl oz/60 ml) heavy cream

2¾ cups (22 fl oz/ 680 ml) whole milk

6 oz (185 g) bittersweet chocolate, finely chopped, plus more for shaving (optional)

1 tsp pure vanilla extract

Whipped Cream (page 214) for serving

makes 6 mini pies

BAKER'S NOTE

You can make this recipe into a 9-inch (23-cm) pie by lining the pan and baking as instructed. Then, pour as much pudding as you can into the shell. You might have a bit of pie dough and pudding left over. You can turn the dough scraps into roll-ups (page 97) and save the pudding in individual custard cups for serving a few days later, once the pie is demolished.

Prepare the flaky pie dough and chill as directed.

Have ready six 5-inch (13-cm) mini pie pans. On a lightly floured work surface, roll out the dough into a circle ¹⁄₁₆–⅛ inch (2–3 mm) thick. Cut out 6 circles, each about 6½ inches (16.5 cm) in diameter. (You will likely be able to cut out only 4 circles, then you'll need to gather the scraps, reroll, and cut out the last 2 circles.) Line the pie pans with the dough. Refrigerate for at least 20 minutes.

Position a rack in the middle of the oven and preheat to 400°F (200°C). Line the pie shells with foil and fill with pie weights or dried beans. Place the pans on a baking sheet and bake until the crusts look dry, about 15 minutes. Remove the foil and weights and bake until the crusts are golden brown, about 13 minutes longer. Remove from the oven.

In a saucepan, whisk together the sugar, cocoa, cornstarch, and salt. Add the cream, whisking until a smooth paste forms. Slowly add the milk and whisk constantly until smooth. Warm the mixture over medium heat, stirring constantly with a heatproof spatula, until the pudding begins to thicken and bubble, about 6 minutes. Add the chocolate and stir until smooth. Stir in the vanilla.

Pour the hot pudding into the crusts and spread evenly (you should have a heaping ½ cup/4 fl oz/125 ml for each). Cover each pie with plastic wrap pressed onto the surface to prevent a skin from forming. Refrigerate for at least 4 hours or, preferably, overnight.

When ready to serve, spread a big dollop of whipped cream atop each pie. Garnish with chocolate shavings, if you like.

BUTTERY BOURBON-PECAN TART

This updated twist on classic pecan pie merges the flavor of toasty pecans with the dark sweetness of brown sugar and bourbon in a thin tart. Serve it with a small glass of the same good-quality bourbon that you use in the filling.

Flaky Pie Dough for single crust (page 212)

⅓ cup (2½ oz/75 g) dark brown sugar

⅓ cup (3 oz/90 g) granulated sugar

⅔ cup (6½ fl oz/ 200 ml) light corn syrup

2 tbsp all-purpose flour

½ tsp kosher salt

2 large eggs

1 large egg yolk

2 tbsp good-quality bourbon

1½ tsp pure vanilla extract

3 tbsp unsalted butter, melted

2 cups (8 oz/250 g) pecan halves

Whipped Cream (page 214) for serving

makes one 10-inch (25-cm) tart

Prepare the flaky pie dough and chill as directed.

In a bowl, whisk together the sugars, corn syrup, flour, salt, whole eggs, egg yolk, bourbon, vanilla, and melted butter. Chill the filling in the refrigerator while you roll out the dough.

On a lightly floured work surface, roll out the dough into a circle about 12 inches (30 cm) in diameter and ⅛ inch (3 mm) thick. Line a 10-inch (25-cm) tart pan with the dough, trimming away any excess dough. Refrigerate until well chilled, about 30 minutes.

Position a rack in the middle of the oven and preheat to 375°F (190°C).

Arrange the pecans in an even layer in the tart shell. Pour the chilled filling evenly over the pecans. Bake until the filling is puffed, brown, and bubbling, about 40 minutes. Let cool completely on a wire rack.

Serve wedges of the tart with big dollops of whipped cream.

BAKER'S NOTE

If you crave a chocolatey pecan pie, sprinkle about ⅓ cup (3 oz/90 g) chocolate chips over the pecans before you pour in the filling, then bake as directed.

CHICKEN, LEEK, AND WILD MUSHROOM POTPIES

Is there anything more down-home than chicken potpie? Stuffed with creamy chicken, butter-sautéed leeks, and earthy mushrooms, this is the gold standard for potpies. Make these pies when you want something hearty and comforting.

Flaky Pie Dough for single crust (page 212)

1 lb (500 g) skin-on, bone-in chicken breasts

2 cups (16 fl oz/500 ml) chicken stock or broth

4 tbsp (2 oz/60 g) unsalted butter

1 carrot, peeled and finely diced

1 leek, white and pale green parts, finely chopped

1 tsp chopped fresh thyme

Kosher salt and freshly ground pepper

½ lb (250 g) mixed wild mushrooms, such as chanterelle, trumpet, or oyster, sliced or chopped

¼ cup (1½ oz/45 g) all-purpose flour

½ cup (4 fl oz/125 ml) whole milk

1 egg, beaten with 1 tsp water

makes 4 potpies

BAKER'S NOTE

For a superclassic potpie, use about half as many button mushrooms and add ½ cup (2½ oz/75 g) frozen peas to the vegetable mixture. You can also top the pies with a square of puff pastry or drop biscuits (see the Note for Beer Rolls, page 67).

Prepare the flaky pie dough and chill as directed.

In a saucepan, combine the chicken and stock and bring to a boil over medium-high heat. Reduce the heat to low, cover, and simmer until the chicken is cooked through, about 20 minutes. Turn off the heat and set aside, covered, for about 10 minutes.

Meanwhile, in a frying pan, melt 1 tablespoon of the butter over medium heat. Add the carrot, leek, thyme, and a pinch of salt and sauté until the vegetables are barely tender, about 1 minute. Add the mushrooms and sauté until the vegetables are tender, about 3 minutes. Transfer to a bowl. Remove the chicken from the stock, discard the skin and bones, and shred the meat into bite-sized pieces into the bowl of vegetables. Season with salt and pepper. Strain the stock into a measuring pitcher; you should have 1¾ cups (14 fl oz/430 ml).

In the frying pan, melt the remaining 3 tablespoons butter over medium heat. Sprinkle the flour over the butter and whisk together until smooth. Cook for about 1 minute. Slowly add the chicken stock, whisking constantly until the mixture is smooth. Whisk in the milk. Let simmer until slightly thickened, 2–3 minutes. Add the chicken-vegetable mixture and stir to combine. Divide among four 1-cup (8–fl oz/250-ml) ramekins.

Position a rack in the middle of the oven and preheat to 425°F (220°C). Line a baking sheet with parchment paper.

On a lightly floured work surface, roll out the dough into a circle about ⅛ inch (3 mm) thick. Cut out 4 rounds of dough, each about ½ inch (12 mm) larger than the diameter of the ramekins. Place a dough round on top of each ramekin and press the edges down over the rim to secure. Cut a few vents in each dough round, then brush each dough round with the egg wash.

Place the ramekins on the prepared sheet. Bake until the crust is golden brown and the filling is bubbly, about 20 minutes. Let cool for about 10 minutes before serving.

GOAT CHEESE, HERB, AND HEIRLOOM TOMATO TART

This is a stunning tart, and it really showcases summer's succulent tomatoes. It's also extremely simple to make, especially if you have pastry at the ready in your freezer. Choose an array of differently colored heirlooms if you can find them.

Flaky Pie Dough for single crust (page 212)

½ lb (250 g) fresh goat cheese, at room temperature

⅓ cup (3 fl oz/80 ml) heavy cream

2 tsp minced fresh herbs, such as basil and chives

3 or 4 heirloom tomatoes, sliced

Kosher salt and freshly ground pepper

2 tbsp roughly chopped fresh basil leaves

½ cup (½ oz/15 g) packed baby or wild arugula leaves

1 tsp olive oil

1 tsp balsamic vinegar

makes one 10-inch (25-cm) tart

Prepare the flaky pie dough and chill as directed.

Position a rack in the middle of the oven and preheat to 400°F (200°C).

On a lightly floured work surface, roll out the dough into a circle about 13 inches (33 cm) in diameter. Transfer the dough to a 10-inch (25-cm) tart pan with a removable bottom and ease into the pan, trimming any excess dough. (Alternatively, roll out the dough into a rectangle and line an 11-by-5½-inch/28-by-14-cm rectangular tart pan.) Line the shell with foil and fill with pie weights or dried beans. Bake until the crust starts to look dry, about 15 minutes. Remove the foil and weights and bake until the crust is golden brown, 5–10 minutes. Let cool.

In a small bowl, beat together the goat cheese and cream until smooth. Stir in the minced herbs. Gently spread the herbed goat cheese over the bottom of the tart shell. Remove the tart shell from the pan and slide onto a flat serving plate.

Lay the tomato slices on the tart so that they are slightly overlapping and in an even layer. Sprinkle with a little salt and pepper. In a small bowl, toss together the basil leaves, arugula, olive oil, and vinegar, and season with salt and pepper. Top the tart with the arugula mixture and serve.

BAKER'S NOTE

Use the juiciest, most colorful tomatoes you can find, and always at the peak of summer freshness. This tart is not worth making in the fall or winter or spring, when tomatoes are not at their best.

CHAPTER SIX

CUSTARDS & SOUFFLÉS

PEAR-CUSTARD TART

The first recipe from Julia Child that I ever made was her French custard apple tart, which I still love to this day. This delicately flavored tart, filled with vanilla-poached pears and brandy-spiked custard and topped with sugary toasted almonds, is an ode to her and that memorable dessert.

Flaky Pie Dough for single crust (page 212)

for the poached pears
¾ cup (6 oz/185 g) sugar

3 ripe but firm pears, preferably Bosc, peeled, quartered, and cored

Peel of 1 orange, removed in strips with a vegetable peeler

½ vanilla bean

1 large egg
¼ cup (2 oz/60 g) sugar plus 1 tbsp

3 tbsp all-purpose flour
½ cup (4 fl oz/125 ml) heavy cream

1 tsp pure vanilla extract or 2 tbsp brandy (optional)

Pinch of kosher salt

¼ cup (1 oz/30 g) sliced almonds, lightly toasted (page 15)

makes one 10-inch (25-cm) tart

BAKER'S NOTE

To turn this into an apple tart, gently sauté 3 peeled, cored, and sliced apples in 1 tablespoon butter until they just start to become tender. Spread evenly in the partially baked crust, pour over the custard, and proceed with the recipe from there.

Prepare the flaky pie dough and chill as directed.

To poach the pears, cut a circle of parchment paper that will fit in a medium saucepan. Cut a small circle in the middle of the parchment. In the saucepan, bring 3 cups (24 fl oz/750 ml) water and the sugar to a boil over high heat. Reduce the heat to medium, then add the pears and orange peel. Split the vanilla bean and scrape out the seeds with the back of a paring knife; add the pod and seeds to the saucepan. Lay the parchment in the saucepan to submerge the pears. Adjust the heat so that the liquid simmers gently and poach the pears until just tender, about 15 minutes. Let cool in the poaching liquid.

Position a rack in the middle of the oven and preheat to 400°F (200°C). On a lightly floured work surface, roll out the dough to a circle about 13 inches (33 cm) in diameter. Transfer the dough to a 10-inch (25-cm) tart pan with a removable bottom and ease into the pan. Trim away any excess dough. Line the tart shell with foil and fill with pie weights or dried beans. Bake until the crust is dried out and just starting to color a bit, about 20 minutes. Remove the foil and weights. Let cool. Reduce the oven temperature to 350°F (180°C).

Cut each pear quarter lengthwise into 4 slices, then lay most of the pear slices in the crust in an overlapping circle close to the rim. Use the remaining slices to fill the middle.

In a bowl, beat together the egg and the ¼ cup sugar until thick and pale. Beat in the flour and then the cream, vanilla, if using, and salt. Pour evenly over the pears. Bake until the custard starts to puff up, about 10 minutes. Sprinkle the toasted almonds and remaining 1 tablespoon sugar over the top of the tart. Continue to bake until the custard is set and lightly browned, 15–20 minutes. Let cool on a wire rack until warm or room temperature before slicing and serving.

CRÈME BRÛLÉE
WITH CARAMELIZED BLOOD ORANGES

If you want a truly magnificent dessert, sure to impress anyone, make this recipe. A thick layer of melt-in-your-mouth vanilla custard is topped with a crackling burnt sugar crust and slices of tart, caramel-coated blood oranges. Swap in regular orange slices if you can't find blood oranges.

3 cups (24 fl oz/ 750 ml) heavy cream	**for the caramelized blood oranges**
½ cup (4 oz/125 g) granulated sugar	2 blood oranges
⅛ tsp kosher salt	¼ cup (2 oz/60 g) granulated sugar
1 vanilla bean	6–8 tsp turbinado sugar
8 large egg yolks	makes 6–8 crème brûlées

BAKER'S NOTE

A kitchen torch gives you control over melting the sugar on top of a crème brulée into a thin layer that can be gleefully shattered with a spoon. A broiler works too, but watch the custards closely and rotate them to melt the sugar evenly.

Position a rack in the middle of the oven and preheat to 300°F (150°C). Have ready 6–8 shallow custard cups or ramekins, each ½–1 cup (4–8 fl oz/125–250 ml), and a baking pan large enough to hold all the cups.

In a saucepan, stir together the cream, granulated sugar, and salt. Split the vanilla bean and scrape out the seeds with the back of a paring knife. Add the seeds and pod to the cream. Bring to a very gentle boil over medium heat, stirring constantly. Turn off the heat, cover, and let stand for 20 minutes.

Meanwhile, in a bowl, whisk the egg yolks just to break them up. Whisking constantly, slowly add the cream mixture to the yolks. Pour through a fine-mesh sieve into a pitcher. Divide the mixture among the custard cups. Place the cups in the baking pan and carefully pour hot water into the pan to reach about halfway up the sides of the cups (I usually add the water once I place the pan on the oven rack). Bake until the custards are just set but still jiggly, 30–35 minutes.

Carefully remove the custards from the water bath, and let cool on a wire rack to room temperature. Cover with plastic wrap pressed directly onto the surface of the custards to prevent a skin from forming. Refrigerate until the custards are thoroughly chilled, at least 2 hours or up to 2 days.

To make the caramelized oranges, trim the ends from each orange, then remove the peel with a paring knife, following the contour of the fruit and making sure to remove all the white pith. Cut each orange crosswise into thin slices, removing any seeds as you go. In a saucepan, stir together the granulated sugar and 2 tablespoons water. Cook over medium-high heat, swirling the pan occasionally, until the syrup turns a deep amber caramel. Immediately remove from the heat, add the orange slices, and swirl the pan to coat them evenly.

Just before serving, preheat the broiler. Sprinkle each custard with about 1 teaspoon of the turbinado sugar, covering the surface with a thin, even layer. Place the custards on a baking sheet and slide into the broiler about 3 inches (7.5 cm) from the heat source. The sugar will melt quickly and caramelize; watch carefully so that the custards do not burn. (You can also melt and caramelize the sugar with a kitchen torch.) Set the custards aside to harden for a few minutes, then top with some of the caramelized oranges.

MEXICAN CARAMEL FLAN

On a trip to Mexico, where my husband and I ate a lot of street food, one of my favorite stands was run by a friendly, motherly woman who sold giant wedges of silky flan, bathed in bittersweet dark caramel. This recipe, with its smooth, creamy, orange-spiked custard, reminds me of her creation.

1¾ cups (14 oz/440 g) sugar

1 tsp light corn syrup

2 cups (16 fl oz/500 ml) whole milk

1 cup (8 fl oz/250 ml) half-and-half

1 tsp finely grated orange zest

Pinch of kosher salt

4 large eggs

1 tsp pure vanilla extract

makes one 9-inch (23-cm) flan

BAKER'S NOTE

To make individual flans, divide the caramel between 6–8 custard cups, then divide the custard between the cups and bake in the water bath as directed. They will take less time to bake than the large flan, so start checking them after about 30 minutes and remove when the custard is slightly set but still a little jiggly.

Have ready a deep 9-inch (23-cm) ceramic or glass pie dish and a large shallow baking pan that will hold the dish.

In a saucepan, combine 1 cup (8 oz/250 g) of the sugar, the corn syrup, and ¼ cup (2 fl oz/60 ml) water and cook over medium heat, stirring occasionally, until the sugar is dissolved, about 3 minutes. Stop stirring and wash down the sugar crystals on the sides of the pan with a pastry brush dipped in water. Continue to cook, swirling the pan occasionally, until the mixture turns a deep golden-brown caramel and starts to steam. You want to make a fairly dark caramel, but be careful that you don't let it burn. Immediately pour the caramel into the pie dish and very carefully swirl to coat the bottom evenly. Set the dish aside. The caramel will cool and harden.

Position a rack in the middle of the oven and preheat to 325°F (165°C).

In a saucepan, warm the milk, half-and-half, orange zest, salt, and remaining ¾ cup (6 oz/185 g) sugar over medium heat until the milk simmers. Cover, remove from the heat, and set aside for a few minutes.

In a bowl, whisk together the eggs and vanilla until combined. Whisking constantly, pour a ladleful of the hot milk mixture into the eggs, then pour the egg mixture into the hot milk mixture in the saucepan, whisking constantly.

Pour the custard through a fine-mesh sieve into the caramel-lined dish. Place the dish in the baking pan and carefully pour hot water into the pan to reach about halfway up the sides of the pie dish. Bake until the custard is mostly set but the center is still jiggly, about 1 hour.

Carefully remove the pie dish from the water bath, place on a wire rack, and let cool to room temperature. Cover with plastic wrap pressed directly onto the surface of the custard to prevent a skin from forming. Refrigerate until chilled, at least 4 hours or up to overnight.

To serve, run a small knife around the inside edge of the dish. Invert a flat serving plate on top of the dish, then invert the dish and plate together. Lift off the dish and cut the flan into wedges.

MILK CHOCOLATE
POTS DE CRÈME

These rich little custards pack a powerful wallop of chocolate and cream. Make sure you don't overbake them, which is important with any custard, but especially so with chocolate custards, as they can turn grainy in a flash.

1 cup (8 fl oz/250 ml) whole milk

¾ cup (6 fl oz/180 ml) heavy cream

4 oz (125 g) excellent-quality dark milk chocolate, coarsely chopped

4 large egg yolks

2 tbsp sugar

Whipped Cream (page 214) for serving

makes 6 pots de crème

BAKER'S NOTE

I've always been a fan of dark, bittersweet chocolate and, until a few years ago, was dismissive of milk chocolate, having only experienced mass-produced types. All that changed when I tried Scharffen Berger's extrarich milk chocolate, which is more flavorful and darker than most. Try to find a good-quality artisan milk chocolate with at least 40 percent cacao for these delicious little puddings.

Position a rack in the middle of the oven and preheat to 325°F (165°C). Have ready six ½-cup (4–fl oz/125-ml) custard cups or ramekins and a shallow baking pan large enough to hold all the cups.

In a small saucepan, heat the milk and cream over medium-low heat until simmering. Add the chopped chocolate and stir until it is melted. In another bowl, whisk together the egg yolks and the sugar until just blended. Gradually whisk the yolks into the chocolate mixture until well blended and smooth. Pour through a fine-mesh sieve into a pitcher.

Divide the chocolate mixture among the cups. Place the cups in the baking pan and carefully pour hot water into the pan to reach halfway up the sides of the cups (I usually add the water once I place the pan on the oven rack). Bake until the custards are just set but still slightly jiggly in the center, about 25 minutes.

Carefully remove the custards from the water bath and transfer to a wire rack; let cool to room temperature. Cover with plastic wrap pressed directly onto the surface of the custards to prevent a skin from forming. Refrigerate until completely chilled, about 3 hours.

Serve with dollops of whipped cream.

FLORIOLE

With firm roots planted in Chicago's Green City Market, Floriole Cafe & Bakery opened its doors in 2010. The popular spot offers a mix of French and American pastries, a great cup of coffee, and a lively atmosphere where regulars can sit and wile away the day.

WHAT DO YOU LOVE ABOUT FLORIOLE?

I love the community we've built over the past few years. Many of our customers have been with us since our first year of selling pastries at the farmers' market. We have seen their kids grow up, welcomed new babies, and in turn, they have seen us expand and open a shop.

WHAT'S THE MOST IMPORTANT LESSON THAT YOU'VE LEARNED?

I'm still learning patience. You can't rush yeasted doughs or toddlers.

WHAT'S YOUR FAVORITE BIRTHDAY TREAT?

Last year my staff surprised me with homemade birthday doughnuts. Much better than cake!

WHAT DO YOU LIKE TO EAT WHEN YOU'RE NOT AT THE BAKERY?

I like to cook simple food at home. Nothing beats a whole roasted chicken, potatoes, and sautéed greens. If we go out to dinner, I love a good pizza from our favorite spot, Great Lake, or a bowl of noodles from Urban Belly.

WHAT'S THE BEST PART ABOUT YOUR CITY?

Free concerts at Millennium Park in the summer, the modern wing of The Art Institute of Chicago, and Chicago-style hot dogs.

FLORIOLE
CANELÉS

*This revered French pastry, a specialty of the Bordeaux region, has a soft custard center
and a dark, caramelized outer crust, and is typically made in its very own mold.
A proper* canéle *is baked until very dark, so don't be afraid of burning them. Bon appétit!*

2 cups (16 fl oz/500 ml) whole milk

¾ cup (6 oz/185 g) plus 2 tbsp sugar

1 vanilla bean

1 cup (5 oz/155 g) all-purpose flour

3½ tbsp unsalted butter, melted

2 large egg yolks

3 tbsp dark rum

¼ tsp kosher salt

makes 8–12 *canelés*

Generously butter 8–12 *canelé* molds and place in the freezer.

In a saucepan, stir together the milk and the sugar. Split the vanilla bean and scrape out the seeds with the back of a paring knife. Add the seeds and pod to the milk. Heat over medium heat until the mixture is steaming. Cover, turn off the heat, and let steep for 20 minutes. Remove the vanilla pod.

Add the flour, butter, egg yolks, rum, and salt and blend with an immersion blender until there are no lumps (or pour into a blender and blend). Transfer the batter to a bowl, cover with plastic wrap, and refrigerate for at least 12 hours or up to 24 hours.

Preheat the oven to 425°F (220°C).

Place the molds on a baking sheet. Whisk the batter and fill the molds within about ⅛ inch (3 mm) of the tops. Bake for 20 minutes. Rotate the baking sheet and bake until the *canelés* are dark golden brown, about 20 minutes. Unmold one to check the color. If it is not dark enough, return it to the mold and continue baking. Immediately unmold the *canelés* onto a wire rack. They will crisp slightly as they cool. They are best eaten the day they are baked.

ORANGE MARMALADE
BREAD AND BUTTER PUDDING

*The first time I made this pudding
and put it in the oven, I had my doubts.
It seemed like a lot of soppy bread in
way too much liquid. But what emerged
after baking was a puffy, golden pudding
that melted in my mouth. This comforting
dessert is gilded with a thin layer
of tangy orange marmalade.*

1 loaf (1 lb/500 g)
challah or brioche,
ends trimmed and
cut into 12 slices

3 tbsp unsalted butter,
at room temperature

3 large eggs

5 large egg yolks

1¾ cups (14 fl oz/
430 ml) whole milk

1 cup (8 fl oz/250 ml)
heavy cream

⅓ cup (3 oz/90 g)
sugar

½ tsp kosher salt

1 tsp pure vanilla extract

Pinch of ground
cinnamon

Pinch of freshly
grated nutmeg

½ cup (5 oz/155 g)
orange marmalade

Whipped Cream
(page 214) for serving

makes about 8 servings

Position a rack in the middle of the oven and preheat to 325°F (165°C). Generously butter a 9-by-13-inch (23-by-33-cm) baking dish.

Spread the challah slices thickly and evenly with the butter. Cut the slices in half crosswise. Lay the slices in the dish so that they overlap slightly.

In a bowl, whisk together the whole eggs, egg yolks, milk, cream, sugar, salt, vanilla, cinnamon, and nutmeg. Pour evenly over the bread. Let stand for about 30 minutes so that the bread soaks up the custard (occasionally press down on the bread for extra absorption).

Bake the pudding for 30 minutes. Meanwhile, gently warm the marmalade in a small saucepan over medium-low heat. Remove the pudding from the oven and carefully spread the marmalade over the top. Return to the oven and bake until the top is crisp, brown, and sticky, about 10 minutes longer. Let stand for about 10 minutes before serving big scoops of the pudding garnished with lightly whipped cream.

BAKER'S NOTE

I like to use eggy challah in bread pudding, as it imparts a great flavor and texture, but you can also use brioche or any other good-quality, somewhat dense white or spiced bread (cinnamon-raisin bread would be good!).

SPICED PERSIMMON
PUDDING

Persimmons seem to arrive all at once, and then, before you know it, they are gone until next year. When you have a glut of the fragrant orange fruits, make this pudding. Richly spiced and very moist, it's best served with fluffy whipped cream.

1½ cups (7½ oz/235 g) all-purpose flour

1 tsp baking powder

¼ tsp baking soda

¾ tsp ground cinnamon

½ tsp ground ginger

¼ tsp freshly grated nutmeg

¼ tsp kosher salt

1¼ cups (11½ oz/360 g) Hachiya persimmon puree (from about 1¼ lb/ 625 g persimmons; see Note)

1 tsp finely grated orange zest

⅔ cup (5 oz/155 g) firmly packed light brown sugar

1 cup (8 fl oz/250 ml) whole milk

6 tbsp (3 oz/90 g) unsalted butter, melted and cooled

3 large eggs

3 tbsp brandy or fresh orange juice

1 tsp pure vanilla extract

Whipped Cream (page 214) for serving

makes about 6 servings

Position a rack in the middle of the oven and preheat to 325°F (165°C). Butter a 9-inch (23-cm) square baking dish.

In a bowl, sift together the flour, baking powder, baking soda, cinnamon, ginger, nutmeg, and salt. In a large bowl, whisk together the persimmon puree, orange zest, brown sugar, milk, butter, eggs, brandy, and vanilla. Gently stir the dry ingredients into the persimmon mixture. Scrape the batter into the prepared dish.

Bake until the pudding is completely set and a toothpick inserted into the center comes out clean, 40–45 minutes. Let cool on a wire rack. Serve warm, at room temperature, or chilled, cut into squares and topped with pillowy dollops of whipped cream.

BAKER'S NOTE

To make persimmon puree, start with very ripe, soft Hachiya persimmons. Trim the top of each, then scoop out the pulp with a spoon. Press the pulp through a medium-mesh sieve placed over a bowl, or put it through a food mill. If you have a lot of persimmons, make the puree and store it by freezing in plastic freezer bags for up to 3 months.

SLOW-BAKED RISOTTO PUDDING

This homespun dessert, delicately flavored with orange zest and cinnamon, couldn't be simpler, and will surely take you back to childhood. Serve the creamy pudding in cute little glass cups, garnished with a sprinkle of cinnamon.

3¾ cups (30 fl oz/ 940 ml) whole milk

¾ cup (5½ oz/170 g) Arborio, Carnaroli, or other short-grain rice

½ cup (4 oz/125 g) sugar

¼ tsp ground cinnamon

Finely grated zest of ½ orange

½ tsp kosher salt

1 large egg yolk, lightly beaten

1 tsp pure vanilla extract

Fig Compote (page 133) or Fruit Compote (page 215) for serving (optional)

makes 4–6 servings

Position a rack in the middle of the oven and preheat to 325°F (165°C). Generously butter a 2-qt (2-l) baking dish.

In a saucepan, whisk together the milk, rice, sugar, cinnamon, orange zest, and salt. Bring to a full boil over medium-high heat (be careful that the mixture doesn't boil over!). Reduce the heat to low and simmer, stirring often, for 1 minute. Whisking constantly, drizzle in the egg yolk, then stir in the vanilla. Carefully pour into the prepared dish.

Cover the dish loosely with foil and poke a few holes in the top of the foil. Bake, stirring about every 15 minutes, until the rice is very tender, about 40 minutes. The mixture will still be a little soupy, but will thicken as it cools.

Remove the foil, set the dish on a wire rack, and let the pudding cool to room temperature, stirring occasionally. Transfer to a serving bowl, cover with plastic wrap, and refrigerate until cold, about 3 hours. Serve big spoonfuls of the pudding with fruit compote, if desired.

BAKER'S NOTE

Risotto rice, such as Arborio, Carnaroli, or Vialone Nano, is a short-grain variety that contains a lot of starch and can absorb a good amount of liquid. When cooked or baked, it is transformed into something creamy and delicious, whether it's a savory risotto or a classic rice pudding.

RICOTTA CHEESECAKE
WITH STRAWBERRY SAUCE

I'm a fan of fresh ricotta, and I often make my own—a process that is surprisingly easy, with a result that tastes extraordinary. Use a good-quality ricotta for this cheesecake, and make sure to process it well so there are no lumps. You'll be rewarded with a deliciously light and creamy cake.

for the crust

3 tbsp sugar, plus more for sprinkling

4 oz (125 g) graham crackers (about 8 crackers)

Pinch of kosher salt

4 tbsp (2 oz/60 g) unsalted butter, melted

for the filling

4 cups (2 lb/1 kg) ricotta cheese

1 cup (8 oz/250 g) sugar

¼ cup (1½ oz/45 g) all-purpose flour

¼ tsp kosher salt

4 large eggs

⅓ cup (2½ oz/75 g) crème fraîche

2 tsp pure vanilla extract

1 tsp finely grated orange zest

for the strawberry sauce

1 pint (8 oz/250 g) strawberries, hulled and sliced

½ cup (4 oz/125 g) sugar

2 tbsp fresh orange juice

2 tbsp fresh lemon juice

makes one 9-inch (23-cm) cheesecake

Position a rack in the middle of the oven and preheat to 350°F (180°C).

To make the crust, generously butter a 9-inch (23-cm) springform pan; sprinkle the sides of the pan with sugar, knocking out the excess. In a food processor, combine the graham crackers, 3 tablespoons sugar, salt, and butter and pulse to form fine crumbs. Press the graham cracker mixture evenly onto the bottom of the pan. Bake until the crust is lightly golden, about 10 minutes. Set aside. Reduce the oven temperature to 325°F (165°C).

To make the filling, in a clean food processor, process the ricotta until smooth and creamy. Add the sugar, flour, and salt and process again until smooth. Scrape down the sides with a rubber spatula as you go. Add the eggs and process until smooth. Add the crème fraîche, vanilla, and orange zest and process until completely combined. Gently pour the filling into the crust-lined pan, being careful not to disturb the crust.

Bake until the filling puffs up slightly and the center jiggles very slightly when the pan is gently shaken, about 1 hour. Transfer to a wire rack and let cool completely, at least 2 hours. You can also refrigerate the cheesecake for up to 2 days before serving.

Meanwhile, make the strawberry sauce: In a saucepan, simmer the strawberries, sugar, and citrus juices over medium-low heat, stirring occasionally, until the strawberries break down and the sauce becomes a bit syrupy, about 6 minutes. Puree the sauce with an immersion blender or in a blender. Let cool completely or refrigerate until ready to use.

To serve, remove the pan sides and slide the cheesecake onto a serving platter. Pour the sauce over the cake, and serve in thick wedges (you can also serve the strawberry sauce alongside the cake).

BAKER'S NOTE

This dessert goes well with just about any kind of fruit. If strawberries are at the peak of their season, skip the sauce and slice them up fresh to serve with the cheesecake. Or, have some fun and serve it with both.

CANNELLE ET VANILLE
RHUBARB CUSTARD
WITH PISTACHIO CRUMBLE

A thick, rich vanilla custard sprinkled with nutty pistachio streusel blankets a hidden layer of tart, lightly poached rhubarb at the bottom of each of these delicious, gluten-free desserts. Be sure to watch the delicate custards carefully as they bake so you don't overcook them.

for the poached rhubarb

½ cup (4 oz/125 g) sugar

4 stalks (4 oz/110 g) rhubarb, cut into 1-inch (2.5-cm) pieces

for the pistachio crumble

¼ cup (1 oz/30 g) unsalted pistachios

4 tbsp (2 oz/60 g) cold unsalted butter, cut into chunks

¼ cup (2 oz/60 g) sugar

¼ cup (1½ oz/45 g) brown rice flour

¼ cup (1½ oz/45 g) almond flour

4½ tsp tapioca flour

Pinch of kosher salt

for the custard

1 vanilla bean

2 cups (16 fl oz/500 ml) heavy cream

½ cup (4 fl oz/125 ml) whole milk

¾ cup (6 oz/185 g) sugar

Grated zest of 1 orange

6 large eggs

¼ cup (1 oz/30 g) cornstarch

makes 8–10 custards

ARAN GOYOAGA
WWW.CANNELLE-VANILLE.BLOGSPOT.COM

Raised in the Basque Region of Northern Spain, Aran Goyoaga was born into a family of bakers. She followed tradition and became a pastry chef herself and is also a self-trained photographer and food stylist. Now living in the U.S., Aran's blog, Cannelle Et Vanille, is treasured in the culinary blogosphere as an inspiring resource for simple, seasonal, gluten-free recipes that are beautifully photographed.

Position a rack in the middle of the oven and preheat to 325°F (160°C). Have ready 8–10 custard cups or ramekins, each at least ¾ cup (6 fl oz/180 ml). Arrange the cups in a baking dish.

To poach the rhubarb, in a small saucepan, combine the sugar and 1 cup (8 fl oz/250 ml) water and heat over medium heat, stirring to dissolve the sugar. Add the rhubarb, reduce the heat so that the sugar syrup is barely simmering, and gently cook the rhubarb until it is soft but still keeps its shape, about 3 minutes. Drain the rhubarb, being careful not to mush it too much.

To make the crumble, finely chop the pistachios in a food processor. Add the butter, sugar, brown rice flour, almond flour, tapioca flour, and salt, and pulse a few times just until a crumbly sandlike dough forms. Transfer to a bowl and refrigerate until ready to use.

To make the custard, split the vanilla bean and scrape out the seeds with the back of a paring knife. In a saucepan, combine the vanilla pod and seeds, the cream, the milk, half of the sugar, and the orange zest. Bring to a boil over medium heat and stir. Remove from the heat and remove the vanilla pod. In a small bowl, whisk together the eggs, cornstarch, and remaining sugar. Pour a little of the hot cream into the egg mixture, a little at a time, and whisk until combined. Strain through a fine-mesh sieve into a pitcher.

Divide the rhubarb between the custard cups. Pour the custard over the rhubarb. Sprinkle the reserved crumble over the top of each custard, dividing it evenly. Carefully pour very hot water into the baking dish to reach about halfway up the sides of the cups. Bake until the custards are set and the crumble is golden, 30–35 minutes. Remove from the water bath, transfer to a wire rack, and let cool completely before serving.

APRICOT-CHERRY CLAFOUTIS

This easy-to-make French custard pancake is often prepared with whole, unpitted cherries, but the addition of apricots gives it a nice tart flavor (and I like to pit the cherries to avoid any chipped teeth!).

3 large eggs

¾ cup (6 fl oz/180 ml) whole milk

¼ cup (2 fl oz/60 ml) heavy cream

6 tbsp (3 oz/90 g) granulated sugar

1 tsp finely grated lemon zest

1 tsp pure vanilla extract

¼ tsp kosher salt

½ cup (2½ oz/75 g) all-purpose flour

2 tbsp unsalted butter

2 apricots, pitted and cut into chunks

1 cup (6 oz/185 g) pitted cherries

Confectioners' sugar for sprinkling

makes 4 servings

Position a rack in the middle of the oven and preheat to 400°F (200°C).

In a blender, combine the eggs, milk, cream, 2 tablespoons of the granulated sugar, the lemon zest, vanilla, salt, and flour. Process until smooth.

In a 10-inch (25-cm) cast-iron pan, melt the butter over medium heat. Stir in 3 tablespoons of the granulated sugar, then add the apricots and cherries. Stir until the mixture becomes syrupy.

Gently pour the egg mixture over the fruit and sprinkle with the remaining 1 tablespoon granulated sugar. Bake until the clafoutis is puffed and golden brown, about 25 minutes. Let cool slightly, dust with confectioners' sugar, and serve.

BAKER'S NOTE

You can bake the clafoutis in a 9-inch (23-cm) cake pan, but cast iron is my favorite. Not only does it give the clafoutis a lovely caramelized crust, but it makes a great serving vessel.

BUTTERSCOTCH CUSTARDS

Butterscotch makes me think of an old-fashioned ice-cream sundae from a charming small-town soda fountain. It's a flavor that doesn't get enough attention, which is a good reason to make these lovely little custards, bursting with the tastes of brown sugar, butter, and a hint of whisky.

3 tbsp unsalted butter

¾ cup (6 oz/185 g) lightly packed dark brown sugar

1½ cups (12 fl oz/ 375 ml) heavy cream

¾ cup (6 fl oz/180 ml) whole milk

5 large egg yolks, lightly beaten

1 tsp pure vanilla extract

1 tbsp whisky, preferably a sweet Scotch (optional)

¼ tsp kosher salt

Whipped Cream (page 214) for serving

makes 6 custards

BAKER'S NOTE

Custards are delicate, and to keep them smooth and silky (and not overbaked and curdled!), it's important to bake them at a low temperature and ideally in a water bath, which helps insulate the custard. Check the custard regularly, and take it out while it still jiggles.

Position a rack in the middle of the oven and preheat to 300°F (150°C). Have ready six ½-cup (4–fl oz/125-ml) custard cups or ramekins and a shallow baking pan large enough to hold all the cups.

In a medium saucepan, melt the butter over medium-low heat. Add the brown sugar and, using a heatproof rubber spatula, stir to combine with the butter. Cook until the sugar starts bubbling like molten lava, about 3 minutes. Stir in the cream, and let it bubble away, stirring with a big whisk until the mixture is smooth and slightly thickened, about 5 minutes. Stir in the milk.

Whisking constantly, slowly pour the egg yolks into the hot cream mixture. Stir in the vanilla, whisky, if using, and salt. Pour the custard through a fine-mesh sieve into a pitcher.

Divide the custard evenly among the custard cups. Place the cups in the baking pan and carefully pour hot water into the pan to reach halfway up the sides of the cups (I add the water once I place the pan on the oven rack). Bake until the custards are set but still jiggle slightly when shaken, 25–30 minutes.

Carefully transfer the baking pan to a wire rack and let the custards cool slightly, then carefully lift the cups out of the water bath. Let the custards cool on the wire rack for 20 minutes. Cover with plastic wrap pressed directly onto the surface of the custards to prevent a skin from forming. Refrigerate until the custards are well chilled, about 4 hours or up to overnight.

Serve cold with dollops of whipped cream.

SAVORY GOAT CHEESE SOUFFLÉS

Be warned: these savory cheese puff soufflés are so light and delicious that you'll have a hard time eating just one. Serve them with a salad made from farmers' market greens tossed with a mustardy vinaigrette for a memorable lunch or supper.

3 tbsp unsalted butter

3 tbsp all-purpose flour

1 cup (8 fl oz/250 ml) whole milk

¾ cup (6 fl oz/180 ml) half-and-half

Kosher salt and freshly ground pepper

3 large egg yolks, lightly beaten

½ lb (250 g) fresh goat cheese

5 large egg whites

1 tbsp chopped fresh flat-leaf parsley

makes 6 soufflés

Position a rack in the lower third of the oven and preheat to 400°F (200°C). Butter and flour six 1-cup (8–fl oz/250-ml) ramekins.

In a saucepan, melt the butter over medium heat. Whisk in the flour and, whisking constantly, let the mixture bubble for about 2 minutes. Slowly drizzle in the milk, whisking constantly to smooth it out. Whisk in the half-and-half. Simmer the mixture, stirring occasionally, until it thickens, about 5 minutes. Remove from the heat. Stir in ¼ teaspoon salt and a generous grinding of pepper. Quickly whisk in the egg yolks until completely blended. Whisk in about three-fourths of the goat cheese until smooth.

In a clean bowl, using a hand mixer, beat the egg whites and a large pinch of salt on medium-high speed to medium-stiff peaks. Spoon about one-third of the beaten whites into the yolk mixture, sprinkle with the remaining goat cheese and the parsley, and stir gently to combine. Using a rubber spatula, fold in the remaining whites.

Divide the mixture among the prepared ramekins and place on a baking sheet. Run a finger around the edge of the soufflé mixture in each ramekin to create a shallow groove. This will create a "top hat" when the soufflés bake. Bake until the soufflés are puffed and golden brown and still a bit wobbly in the center, 20–25 minutes. Serve while hot, before they fall!

BAKER'S NOTE

When beating egg whites, start with a clean bowl free of any grease or fat. I find it best to use an electric mixer, unless you want to get a workout with a handheld whisk. Beat the egg whites on medium-high speed until the whites barely curl on themselves when you lift the whip. Do not to overbeat the whites, or they will become grainy.

CHEESY SOUTHERN
SPOON BREAD

Deeply southern in its roots, spoon bread is like a corn bread pudding in soufflé form. It's great served alongside many southern entrées such as baked ham, fried chicken, or a hearty chile con carne. As the name indicates, use a big spoon to serve it.

2½ cups (20 fl oz/ 625 ml) whole milk

½ tsp salt

½ cup (2½ oz/75 g) fine cornmeal

4 tbsp (2 oz/60 g) unsalted butter, cut into chunks

6 large eggs, separated

1 cup (4 oz/125 g) shredded sharp Cheddar cheese

makes 8–10 servings

Position a rack in the middle of the oven and preheat to 350°F (180°C). Butter a 9-by-13-inch (23-by-33-cm) baking dish.

In a saucepan, combine the milk and salt. Bring to a slow boil over medium-high heat. When bubbles appear along the sides of the pan, reduce the heat to a simmer. Stir in the cornmeal and cook, stirring, until it thickens, about 4 minutes. Stir in the butter. In a small bowl, whisk together the egg yolks. Remove from the heat and whisk the egg yolks and cheese into the cornmeal mixture. Let cool slightly.

In a clean bowl, using a hand mixer, beat the egg whites on medium-high speed to medium peaks. Gently fold the beaten whites into the cornmeal mixture just until no white streaks are visible. Scrape into the prepared dish. (The spoon bread can be prepared up to this point, covered, and refrigerated for up to 8 hours; bring to room temperature before baking.)

Bake until the spoon bread is puffed and golden brown, about 30 minutes. Serve while it's hot.

BAKER'S NOTE

Use a gentle hand when folding beaten egg whites into a batter. First lighten the batter by stirring in about one-fourth of the whites. Then scrape the rest of the whites on top of the batter and, using a rubber spatula and starting in the middle, gently fold them in using a scooping motion while rotating the bowl. Only fold the whites until there are no more streaks, and be sure not to overfold.

BITTERSWEET CHOCOLATE–
RASPBERRY SOUFFLÉS

Dig down to the bottom of these ethereal chocolate soufflés and you'll find a layer of fresh, tart raspberries to liven up your taste buds. My family practically licked the ramekins clean when I made these elegant little desserts for them.

7 tbsp (3½ oz/105 g) granulated sugar, plus more for coating

1 cup (4 oz/125 g) raspberries

3 tbsp unsalted butter

6 oz (185 g) bittersweet chocolate, finely chopped

½ tsp pure vanilla extract

5 large eggs, separated, plus 2 egg whites

Pinch of kosher salt

¼ tsp cream of tartar

Confectioners' sugar for dusting

makes 6 soufflés

BAKER'S NOTE

Whenever you bake something where any form of chocolate is the prevalent flavor, use an excellent-quality chocolate, such as Valrhona from France, El Rey from Venezuela, or a local artisan brand like Recchiuti from San Francisco or Payard from New York. It will make a difference in the finished dessert.

Position a rack in the lower third of the oven and preheat to 375°F (190°C). Butter six 1 cup (8–fl oz/250-ml) ramekins and dust with granulated sugar. In a small bowl, toss the raspberries with 1 tablespoon of the granulated sugar and divide among the ramekins.

In a small saucepan, melt the butter and chocolate over low heat, stirring until smooth. Remove from the heat and stir in the vanilla. In the bowl of a mixer fitted with the whip attachment, beat together the egg yolks and 3 tablespoons of the granulated sugar on medium speed until thick and fluffy. Fold the chocolate mixture into the egg yolks.

In a clean bowl or bowl of a mixer, using clean beaters or the whip attachment, beat the egg whites, salt, and cream of tartar on medium-high speed until foamy. Add the remaining 3 tablespoons granulated sugar and beat to thick, glossy, stiff peaks.

Fold the beaten whites into the chocolate mixture. Divide the mixture among the ramekins. Run a finger around the edge of the soufflé mixture in each ramekin to create a shallow groove. This will create a "top hat" when the soufflés bake. (The soufflés can be prepared up to this point, covered with plastic wrap, and refrigerated for up to 1 day.)

Place the soufflés on a rimmed baking sheet. Bake until the soufflés are set and puffed and the center still jiggles when the ramekins are shaken, about 20 minutes. Dust with confectioners' sugar and serve right away, before they fall!

BASIC RECIPES

FLAKY PIE DOUGH: SINGLE CRUST

1¼ cups (6½ oz/200 g) all-purpose flour

¼ tsp kosher salt

½ tsp sugar (optional; omit if making a savory dish)

7 tbsp (3½ oz/105 g) very cold unsalted butter, cut into cubes

5 tbsp (3 fl oz/80 ml) ice water, plus more if needed

makes enough for one 9-inch (23-cm) pie or tart

In the bowl of a food processor, stir together the flour, salt, and sugar, if using. Sprinkle the butter over the top and pulse for a few seconds, or just until the butter is slightly broken up into the flour but still in visible pieces. Evenly sprinkle the water over the flour mixture, then process just until the mixture starts to come together. Dump the dough into a large lock-top plastic bag, and press into a flat disk. Refrigerate the dough for 30 minutes or up to 1 day, or freeze for up to 1 month.

FLAKY PIE DOUGH: DOUBLE CRUST

2 cups (10 oz/315 g) all-purpose flour

½ tsp kosher salt

1 tsp sugar (optional; omit if making a savory dish)

¾ cup (6 oz/185 g) very cold unsalted butter, cut into cubes

8 tbsp (4 fl oz/125 ml) ice water, plus more if needed

makes enough for one 9-inch (23-cm) double-crust pie or two 9-inch (23-cm)single-crust tarts or pies or six 5-inch (13-cm) mini pies

In the bowl of a food processor, stir together the flour, salt, and sugar, if using. Sprinkle the butter over the top and pulse for a few seconds, or just until the butter is slightly broken up into the flour but still in visible pieces. Evenly sprinkle the water over the flour mixture, then process just until the mixture starts to come together. Dump the dough onto a work surface, press it together, then divide it in half. Press each half into a disk, then place the disks in a large lock-top plastic bag. Refrigerate the dough for 30 minutes or up to 1 day, or freeze for up to 1 month.

VANILLA CHIFFON CAKE

2 cups (8 oz/250 g) cake flour

2 tsp baking powder

1 cup (8 oz/250 g) sugar

⅓ cup (3 fl oz/80 ml) canola oil

2 tsp pure vanilla extract

4 large eggs, separated

½ tsp kosher salt

¼ tsp cream of tartar

makes two 9-inch (23-cm) cake layers

Preheat the oven to 350°F (180°C). Butter two 9-by-2-inch (23-by-5-cm) round cake pans and line the bottoms with parchment paper. Butter the paper and dust with flour. In a bowl, sift together the flour and baking powder. Whisk in ½ cup (4 oz/125 g) of the sugar. In another bowl, whisk together the oil, vanilla, egg yolks, and ⅓ cup (3 fl oz/80 ml) plus 2 tablespoons water. In a third bowl, using a mixer with the whip attachment, beat the egg whites, salt, and cream of tartar. When the egg whites get frothy, slowly add the remaining ½ cup sugar, beating until stiff peaks form. Whisk the dry ingredients into the wet ingredients, then fold the egg whites into the batter. Divide the batter between the prepared pans. Bake until a toothpick inserted into the centers comes out clean, 15–18 minutes. Let cool completely in the pans on a wire rack before unmolding. If you like, you can freeze the layers: wrap each with plastic wrap, place in a large lock-top plastic freezer bag, and freeze for up to 1 month. Thaw before using.

BAKED'S FLOURLESS CHOCOLATE CAKE

4 tbsp (2 oz/60 g) unsalted butter

6 oz (185 g) dark chocolate, chopped

2 tbsp plus 1 tsp instant espresso powder

¼ cup (2 fl oz/60 ml) strong brewed coffee, at room temperature

¼ tsp kosher salt

1 tbsp pure vanilla extract

6 large eggs, separated, at room temperature

1 cup (8 oz/250 g) sugar

makes one 9-inch (23-cm) cake

Melt the butter and the chocolate in a heatproof bowl set over (not touching) simmering water in a saucepan. Remove from the heat and whisk until smooth. Let cool. In a small bowl, whisk together the espresso powder, coffee, salt, and vanilla. In the bowl of a stand mixer fitted with the whisk attachment, beat the egg yolks with ½ cup (4 oz/125 g) of the sugar on medium-high speed until the mixture is light and has almost doubled in volume, about 5 minutes. Add the chocolate mixture and beat until just combined. Reduce the speed to low, add the coffee mixture, and beat until just combined. In a clean bowl, using the whisk attachment, beat the egg whites on medium-high speed until foamy. Gradually raise the speed to high, add the remaining ½ cup sugar, and beat until soft peaks form. Scoop 1 cup (8 fl oz/ 250 ml) of the egg whites into the chocolate mixture and gently fold in using a rubber spatula. After about 30 seconds of folding, add the remaining egg whites and fold in until almost completely combined. Take care not to overmix. Use as directed in the Mississippi Mud Pie recipe (page 159) or pour into a buttered 9-inch (23-cm) springform pan lined with buttered parchment paper and bake at 350°F (180°C) until the cake is set but still jiggles slightly, about 40 minutes. Transfer to a wire rack and let cool completely.

VANILLA MERINGUE BUTTERCREAM

The buttercream comes together quickly, so have all your ingredients measured and at the ready. Don't worry—making this might seem intimidating at first, but once you get the hang of it, you'll find it's really quite fun. You will need a candy thermometer. A stand mixer is best.

9 large egg whites

½ tsp cream of tartar

¼ tsp salt

½ cup (4 oz/125 g) sugar plus 1⅔ cup (13 oz/410 g)

2 tsp corn syrup

3 cups (1½ lb/750 g) unsalted butter, at room temperature, cut into chunks

1 tbsp pure vanilla extract

makes more than enough to frost a double layer cake or 12–18 cupcakes

In the bowl of a stand mixer fitted with the whip attachment, combine the egg whites, cream of tartar, and salt. Beat the egg whites on high speed until foamy.

Continuing to beat, start adding the ½ cup sugar in a very slow, steady stream. When the egg whites are at medium peak, turn the mixer to low speed to continue stirring the meringue while you boil the sugar syrup.

In a saucepan, stir together the 1⅔ cup sugar and ⅓ cup (3 fl oz/80 ml) water. Add the corn syrup. Bring the mixture to a boil over medium-high heat, swirling the pan occasionally at first until the sugar is dissolved. Fit the pan with a candy thermometer and boil until the syrup reaches 245°F (118°C) or the "firm-ball" stage. Immediately return the mixer to high speed and whip the whites to firm peaks, just a few seconds more. Turn the mixer to medium speed, and very carefully, in a steady stream, pour the sugar syrup into the meringue, trying your best not to let the syrup touch the sides of the bowl or the whip. Continue beating the meringue on medium-low speed until the mixture cools down a bit, about 15–20 minutes. It will expand.

When the bottom of the bowl is nearly room temperature, slowly start adding the butter in pieces. Once all the butter has been added, turn the mixer to high speed and beat until the mixture is creamy. At first, it will look chunky and as if it has separated, but keep whipping until the buttercream becomes smooth and lustrous. Add the vanilla and beat until smooth. Use right away, or cover and refrigerate for up to 1 day; bring to room temperature before using.

Variations

Chocolate: Stir in 4 oz (125 g) melted and cooled bittersweet chocolate along with the vanilla after you whip in the butter. Beat until smooth and creamy.

Espresso: Omit the vanilla. Dissolve 2 tablespoons instant espresso powder in 2 teaspoons hot water. Let cool. Stir in after you whip in the butter. Beat until smooth and creamy.

Caramel: Stir in ¼–½ cup (2–4 fl oz/60–125 ml) *dulce de leche* along with the vanilla after you whip in the butter. Beat until smooth and creamy.

Lemon: Stir in ¼–½ cup (2–4 fl oz/60–125 ml) lemon curd (page 215) along with the vanilla after you whip in the butter. Beat until smooth and creamy.

7-MINUTE FROSTING

3 large egg whites, at room temperature

¾ cup (6 oz/185 g) sugar

2 tbsp light corn syrup

⅛ tsp kosher salt

1 tsp pure vanilla extract

makes enough to frost a double layer cake or 12–18 cupcakes

In a heatproof bowl, whisk together the egg whites, sugar, corn syrup, salt, and ⅓ cup (3 fl oz/80 ml) water. Set the bowl over (but not touching) barely simmering water in a saucepan. Using a hand mixer, beat on medium-high speed to stiff peaks, about 5 minutes. Remove the bowl from over the water and continue to beat until the mixture cools, about 2 minutes. Add the vanilla and beat until blended. This frosting does not keep well, so use it right away.

CREAM CHEESE FROSTING

½ lb (250 g) cream cheese, at room temperature

4 tbsp (2 oz/60 g) unsalted butter, at room temperature

2 tsp pure vanilla extract

1 cup (4 oz/125 g) confectioners' sugar, sifted

makes enough to frost about 12 cupcakes

In the bowl of a mixer fitted with the paddle attachment, beat the cream cheese, butter, and vanilla on medium-high speed until light and fluffy, about 2 minutes. Gradually beat in the sugar and continue to mix until thoroughly combined, scraping down the sides of the bowl as needed. Use right away, or if the consistency is too soft, refrigerate the frosting until it is spreadable, about 15 minutes. The frosting will keep in the refrigerator for up to 3 days before using.

WHIPPED CREAM

1 cup (8 fl oz/250 ml) heavy cream

1 tbsp sugar, or more to taste

1 tsp pure vanilla extract

makes about 2 cups (16 fl oz/500 ml) whipped cream

In the bowl of a mixer fitted with the whip attachment, add the cream, sugar to taste, and vanilla. Beat on medium-high speed until medium peaks form. Don't overwhip the cream, or it will become stiff and grainy. Serve right away or cover with plastic wrap and serve within 2 hours; fluff the cream with a whisk before serving.

VANILLA GLAZE

½ cup (2 oz/60 g) confectioners' sugar

1 tsp pure vanilla extract

1 tsp whole milk

makes about ½ cup (4 fl oz/125 ml) glaze

In a small bowl, stir together the confectioners' sugar, vanilla, and milk until smooth. Use right away. If the glaze starts to harden, add a few drops of water and stir until the desired consistency is reached.

CITRUS GLAZE

1 cup (4 oz/125 g) confectioners' sugar

1 tbsp lemon juice

1 tbsp orange juice

makes about 1 cup (8 fl oz/250 ml) glaze

In a medium bowl, stir together the confectioners' sugar and citrus juices until smooth. Use right away. If the glaze starts to harden, add a few drops of water and stir until the desired consistency is reached.

RASPBERRY JAM

1 large Granny Smith apple

2 pints (1 lb/500 g) raspberries

1 cup (8 oz/250 g) sugar

2 tbsp fresh lemon juice

makes about 2 cups (1¼ lb/625 g) jam

Place a saucer in the freezer to chill. Have ready a small stainless steel bowl set in a bowl of ice water. Shred the apple, including the skin, on the large holes of a box grater; discard the core and seeds.

In a saucepan, combine the shredded apple, raspberries, sugar, and lemon juice. Bring to a boil over medium heat, stirring constantly to dissolve the sugar. Reduce the heat to medium-low and cook uncovered, stirring occasionally, until the berries are tender and the juices thicken, 10 minutes.

To test, remove the chilled saucer from the freezer. Spoon about 1 teaspoon of the berry mixture onto the saucer and let stand for 15 seconds. If the liquid thickens to a jamlike consistency, the jam is ready. If not, continue to cook for a few minutes longer. Transfer the jam to the bowl set over ice water and let stand until cooled and thickened. Store in the refrigerator for up to 2 weeks.

FRUIT COMPOTE

2 cups (10 oz/315 g) peeled, pitted, and cut-up ripe, seasonal fruit, such as peaches, nectarines, plums, cherries, apples, pears, strawberries, blackberries, or rhubarb

2 tsp fresh lemon juice

About ¼ cup (2 oz/60 g) sugar, or to taste, depending on the sweetness of the fruit

makes about 2 cups (16 fl oz/500 ml) compote

In a saucepan, combine the fruit, lemon juice, and sugar. Simmer over medium heat, stirring occasionally, until the fruit becomes juicy and is just tender. The timing will depend upon the variety of fruit. For example, you'll likely only need to cook berries for a few minutes, but apples or rhubarb will take longer to soften and release their juices. Remove from the heat and set aside to cool. Serve warm or refrigerate and serve chilled. The compote will keep for up to 1 week in the refrigerator.

LEMON CURD

1 large egg

4 large egg yolks

½ cup (4 oz/125 g) sugar

⅓ cup (3 fl oz/80 ml) fresh lemon juice, strained

2 tbsp unsalted butter

makes about 1 cup (8 fl oz/250 ml) lemon curd

In a heatproof bowl set over (but not touching) barely simmering water in a saucepan, whisk together the whole egg, egg yolks, sugar, and lemon juice. Cook, stirring constantly, until thickened, about 5 minutes. Remove from the heat and add the butter, stirring until incorporated. Strain into another bowl. Cover with a piece of plastic wrap pressed directly on top of the curd and refrigerate until chilled. The curd will keep for about 1 week in the refrigerator.

HONEY BUTTER

4 tbsp (2 oz/60 g) unsalted butter, at room temperature

2 tbsp good-quality honey

Kosher salt to taste

makes about ¼ cup (2 oz/60 g) honey butter

In a bowl, combine the butter, honey, and salt to taste. Using a hand mixer, beat together until creamy and fluffy, about 2 minutes. Store in the refrigerator, wrapped in plastic wrap, until ready to use.

GLAZED PECANS

1 tbsp unsalted butter

1 cup (4 oz/125 g) chopped pecans

¼ cup (2 oz/60 g) sugar

makes 1 cup (5 oz/150 g)

Line a rimmed baking sheet with parchment paper. In a nonstick frying pan, melt the butter over medium heat. Add the pecans and cook, stirring constantly, until lightly toasted, about 4 minutes. Add the sugar and stir to coat evenly. Add 1 tablespoon water (be careful, as the mixture might spit and hiss at you). Cook, stirring constantly, until the water evaporates, the sugar melts, and the mixture gets sticky, about 3 minutes. Be careful that the mixture doesn't burn. Spread the glazed pecans on the prepared sheet and let cool before using.

PIZZA SAUCE

1 can (28 oz/875 g) crushed tomatoes (my favorite are 6 in 1 Tomatoes if you can find them)

1 tsp finely chopped fresh herbs such as oregano, basil, or marjoram

1 tbsp balsamic vinegar

Salt and freshly ground pepper

makes enough for 4 pizzas

In a bowl, stir together the tomatoes, herbs, and vinegar. Add 1 teaspoon salt and season with pepper. If you like your sauce smooth, use an immersion blender to blend it a few times. Taste and add more salt and pepper as needed. You do not need to cook this sauce, as it will cook on the pizzas. Store in the refrigerator for up to 1 week or in the freezer for up to 1 month.

TIPS & TRICKS TO MAKING
YOUR BAKING LIFE EASIER

Here are a handful of techniques that you'll likely use again and again when you bake.
Some of these are pretty straightforward, and others take a bit of practice.

MEASURING INGREDIENTS

Measuring ingredients accurately is certainly important when baking, but don't worry if you accidentally splash a little extra vanilla extract into the bowl or a teaspoon of flour falls to the side when you are mixing batter. A bit here and there is probably not going to make much difference. What is important is to remember to measure items in the appropriate vessels, as dry ingredient and liquid ingredient measuring cups are not interchangeable.

SIFTING DRY INGREDIENTS

I like to sift my dry ingredients—it removes any lumps or clumps, it aerates the ingredients, and it helps mix them together. Ideally, use a two- or three-screen sifter. Just place it over your mixing bowl or on top of a piece of parchment paper and add the dry ingredients according to your recipe. If you don't have a sifter, just use a fine-mesh sieve. Add the ingredients to the sifter or sieve, then gently tap the edge to encourage the ingredients to fall into the bowl or onto the paper.

CREAMING BUTTER AND SUGAR

A lot of recipes for cookies, quickbreads, and cakes call for creaming the butter and sugar together, which adds air to the butter to encourage a light-textured finished treat. Try to use butter that is at cool room temperature; avoid using butter that is hard as a rock, or almost melting. Cut it into chunks, about ½ inch in size, then add the chunks to a mixing bowl. Fit a stand mixer with a paddle attachment or a handheld mixer with the beater attachments and beat the butter for a minute or so just to loosen it up. Add the sugar in a stream, then beat it on medium-high speed, scraping down the sides of the bowl with a rubber spatula, until the mixture is lightened in color and fluffy. It should take about 3 minutes.

WHIPPING EGG WHITES

Whipping egg whites can be a little bit tricky, but don't let that daunt you. The key is to make sure you don't overwhip. It's best to separate your egg whites and yolks while the eggs are still cold, as it's easier to do and there's less chance of bursting the yolk. But you'll want the egg whites to be room tempurature for the loftiest whip. To warm them, put the egg whites in a mixing bowl and set that bowl into a larger bowl filled with very warm water. Swirl the egg whites around to warm them slightly.

When you are ready to whip the egg whites, fit a stand mixer or handheld mixer with a whip attachment. Beat the egg whites on medium-high speed (I often add a pinch of cream of tartar to help stabilize them, depending on what the recipe suggests; you can also use a copper bowl and omit the cream of tartar) until the whites become foamy. This is the time to start adding the sugar, if the recipe calls for it, in a slow, steady stream.

If the recipe calls for egg whites whipped to medium peaks, continue to beat them on medium-high speed until the whites are fluffy and opaque but still slightly moist. They should have a slightly curved peak on top when the whip is lifted from the bowl, like what you'd see on a soft-serve ice cream cone.

If the recipe calls for egg whites whipped to stiff peaks, continue to beat until the whites look glossy. When the whip is lifted, they should hold a straight peak. Be extra careful not to overbeat, or they will become grainy.

FOLDING EGG WHITES INTO A BATTER

Once you've beaten your egg whites, it's best not to let them sit before folding them in to your batter (they'll start to firm up and leech liquid). Using a large rubber spatula, plop about a quarter of the whipped whites into the batter and gently stir it in; this lightens the mixture. Scrape the rest of the whipped egg whites on top of the batter.

To fold, using the spatula, slice down through the center of the egg white and batter to the bottom of the bowl, then pull the spatula toward the edge of the bowl and, keeping the flat side against the bottom and side of the bowl, pull it up the side and over the top, bringing some of the batter with it. Rotate the bowl a quarter turn and repeat. Continue folding in this manner just until the whipped egg whites are incorporated into the batter. Be careful not to overfold the mixture or you'll lose all that hard-earned air and it will deflate. Don't worry, a little streaking is fine.

CUTTING A CAKE INTO LAYERS

Once you've baked your beautiful cake, inverted them out of the pans onto wire racks, and let them cool completely, you are ready to gussy them up with filling and frosting.

Before I get started, I like to have a few cardboard cake circles on hand. They give the base of the cake extra stability, and make moving thin cake layers around a lot more easy. Just cut out 2–3 rounds of cardboard that are each the same diameter as your cake layers. Place one cardboard round onto a flat surface and top it with a cake layer.

To cut the cakes into thin layers, hold a ruler vertically against the side of the cake and, using toothpicks, mark the midpoint at regular intervals around the cake. Using a long, thin serrated knife, split the cake in half horizontally, using the toothpicks as a guide, and turning the cake while you cut (it's even easier if you have a turntable). Slide the top layer onto another cardboard circle. Repeat with another cake layer if you need to, setting all the layers except for the base layer off to the side while you start filling the layers.

FILLING CAKE LAYERS

To fill cake layers, place the bottom cake layer on a cardboard cake circle (if you haven't already; see above) and place on a cake decorating turntable or work surface. If you don't have a cardboard cake circle, place the bottom cake layer on a flat serving platter or cake stand.

Using a flat icing spatula or an offset spatula, mound a portion of the filling (all of it if you have a double-layer cake, half of it if you have a triple-layer cake, as so on) in the center of the cake layer and gently spread it just to the edge. I find that turning the cake slowly while spreading the filling is helpful, which is easy to do if you have a decorating turntable.

Carefully place another layer onto the filling (cut side up if you've cut it into layers, or top side down if not). Gently push the layer evenly into place, lining up the edges. Now you are ready to frost the cake.

FROSTING A CAKE

Before frosting or glazing a cake, I like to make a crumb coating, which is a thin layer of frosting that sticks all the crumbs to the cake so they don't get mixed up in the finished layer of frosting. Make sure your filled layer cake is on a turntable, work surface, a serving platter, or a cake stand. Put a small amount of frosting (no more than a third) on top of the cake. Using an icing spatula, smooth a thin layer of frosting over the whole cake. The crumb coating should be a very thin, even layer that covers the entire surface of the cake. Refrigerate the cake until the frosting is firm, 15–30 minutes.

If you haven't already, place the filled cake (still on its cardboard cake circle) on a serving platter or cake stand. Cut 4 strips of parchment paper or aluminum foil, and tuck a strip under each side of the cake to protect the plate from drips. If you want to use some of the frosting to decorate the cake later, set a bit aside before you begin. Mound half of the remaining frosting in the center of the cake and, using an icing spatula, smooth it gently and evenly over the top. Smooth the remaining half of the frosting over the sides of the cake, using broad strokes and holding the spatula nearly perpendicular to the top. Try not to touch the spatula to the cake unless you have it covered with frosting, or you might pick up some stray crumbs from the cake.

To smooth out the frosting, wipe the spatula clean, then hold the spatula parallel to the top and sweep it across the top. Voila! A beautiful, frosted cake!

ROLLING OUT PIE DOUGH

After making pie dough, let it rest for a little while in the refrigerator, as it ensures that the chunks of butter stay cold, and it gives the moisture a chance to disperse throughout the dough.

Remove the chilled dough disk(s) from the refrigerator. If the dough is too cold and firm to roll out, let it stand at room temperature for about 10 minutes (or less if it's a really warm day, you don't want your dough to get overly warm). Dust a flat work surface and a rolling pin with flour. Place a dough disk in the center of the work surface.

Starting from the center and rolling toward the edges and in all directions, roll out the dough into a round. For a 9-inch pie or tart, I usually roll mine out to about 12 inches (30 cm) in diameter and about ⅛ inch (3 mm) thick. Use firm pressure and work quickly to prevent the dough from becoming too warm. If it does start to get overly warm and floppy, carefully slide it onto a baking sheet and refrigerate for a few minutes to let it chill out.

As you roll the dough, lift and rotate it several times to make sure it doesn't stick to the work surface, dusting the surface and the rolling pin with flour as needed. I also like to flip the whole disk over occasionally, especially when I first start rolling, as it helps to keep the dough smooth. If the dough does stick, carefully loosen it with a bench scraper or a plastic scraper (see page 10), lightly flour the work surface, and continue to roll. Don't worry if it tears slightly, just squish it back together and continue rolling.

LINING A PIE OR TART PAN

When you are ready to line your pie or tart pan, gently roll the round of dough loosely around the rolling pin and then unroll it over the pie or tart pan so that it is roughly centered on the pan. Lift the edges of the dough up to allow the dough to settle into the bottom and sides of the pan evenly, being careful not to stretch or tear the dough. Trim the dough to leave a small overhang. I usually like to leave about a 1-inch overhang, but it will depend on your recipe.

FLUTING AND CRIMPING PIE DOUGH

To finish the edge of the dough, for a single-crust pie, fold the overhang underneath itself so that it is even with the edge of the pan. For a double-crust pie, fold the top and bottom dough edges together underneath themselves.

To flute the dough edge, pinch the folded edge between the index finger of one hand and the index finger and thumb of your other hand all the way around the edge of the pie pan, spacing your fingers evenly to form pretty scallops.

To crimp the dough edge, use a fork to press down and make an imprint on the edge of the dough all the way around the circumference of the pan.

KNEADING YEAST DOUGH

Kneading yeast dough is an important step in the bread-making process. Kneading helps develop the gluten in the dough and ensures you have light, springy breads. Using a stand mixer and a dough hook makes this whole process much easier, but if you don't have one, or if you just want a good workout, you can knead the dough by hand.

Make sure you have a sturdy work surface that is at a comfortable height and allows for easy arm movement at the elbows. Lightly flour the surface, then turn out the shaggy bread dough. Using the heel of one or both hands, push the dough away from you. Pull back the far end of the dough, folding it over on itself. Rotate the dough a quarter turn and repeat the steps, pressing the dough, folding it over, and turning it repeatedly. It should become a fluid motion.

As you are kneading, add small amounts of flour to prevent the dough from becoming overly sticky, allowing the flour to be absorbed into the dough before adding more. If necessary, use a bench scraper or plastic scraper to help lift the dough cleanly from the floured surface. Knead until the dough is smooth and elastic, 8–12 minutes, then form it into a ball and let it rise according to the recipe.

VOLUME

SPOONS & CUPS	FLUID OUNCES	MILLILITERS
1 tsp		5 ml
½ tbsp (1½ tsp)		7.5 ml
1 tbsp (3 tsp)	½ fl oz	15 ml
2 tbsp	1 fl oz	30 ml
¼ cup (4 tbsp)	2 fl oz	60 ml
⅓ cup (5 tbsp)	2½ fl oz	75 ml
½ cup	4 fl oz	125 ml
⅔ cup	5 fl oz	150 ml
¾ cup	6 fl oz	175 ml
1 cup	8 fl oz	250 ml
2 cups (1 US pint)	16 fl oz	500 ml
4 cups (1 quart)	32 fl oz	950 ml

WEIGHT

OUNCES/POUNDS	GRAMS/KILOGRAMS
½ oz	15 g
1 oz	30 g
2 oz	60 g
3 oz	90 g
4 oz	115 g
5 oz	150 g
6 oz	175 g
7 oz	200 g
8 oz (½ lb)	225 g
9 oz	250 g
10 oz	300 g
11 oz	325 g
12 oz	350 g
13 oz	375 g
14 oz	400 g
15 oz	425 g
16 oz (1 lb)	450 g
32 oz (2 lb)	900 g
2¼ lb	1 kg

VOLUME OF STANDARD BAKING PANS

PAN	DIMENSIONS	VOLUME
Square	8 x 8 x 1½ inches	6 cups
	8 x 8 x 2 inches	8 cups
	9 x 9 x 2 inches	10 cups
	10 x 10 x 2 inches	12 cups
	12 x 12 x 2 inches	16 cups
Rectangular	11 x 7 x 2 inches	8 cups
	13 x 9 x 2 inches	12 cups
Jelly Roll	10½ x 15½ x 1 inch	10 cups
Loaf	8 x 4 x 2½ inches	4 cups
	8½ x 4½ x 2½ inches	6 cups
	9 x 5 x 3 inches	8 cups
Round	6 x 2 inches	3¾ cups
	8 x 1½ inches	4 cups
	8 x 2 inches	7 cups
	9 x 1½ inches	6 cups
	9 x 2 inches	8½ cups
	10 x 2 inches	10¾ cups
	12 x 2 inches	15½ cups
	14 x 2 inches	21 cups
Springform	9 x 2¾ inches	10 cups
	9 x 3 inches	12 cups
	10 x 2¾ inches	12 cups
Bundt	9 x 3 inches	9 cups
	10 x 3½ inches	12 cups
Tube	9 x 3 inches	10 cups
	10 x 4 inches	16 cups

OVEN TEMPERATURES

°F	°C	GAS
250°	130°	½
275°	140°	1
300°	150°	2
325°	170°	3
350°	180°	4
375°	190°	5
400°	200°	6
425°	220°	7
450°	230°	8
475°	250°	9

INDEX

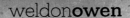

weldon**owen**

415 Jackson Street, Suite 200, San Francisco, CA 94111
www.weldonowen.com

Weldon Owen is a division of
BONNIER

HOME BAKED COMFORT

Conceived and produced by Weldon Owen, Inc.
In collaboration with Williams-Sonoma, Inc.
3250 Van Ness Avenue, San Francisco, CA 94109

Color separations by Mission Productions in Hong Kong
Printed and bound in China by 1010 Printing Ltd

This edition printed in 2014
10 9 8 7 6 5 4 3 2 1

Library of Congress Cataloging-in-Publication
data is available

ISBN-13: 978-1-61628-824-2
ISBN-10: 1-61628-824-8

A WELDON OWEN PRODUCTION

First edition copyright © 2011 Weldon Owen, Inc.
and Williams-Sonoma, Inc.

This edition copyright © 2014

Photographer, Food and Prop Stylist **Eric Wolfinger**
Assistant Food Stylist **Julieann Moore**
Photographer's Assistant **Kelly Puleio**

ACKNOWLEDGMENTS

From Kim Laidlaw: A huge thanks to all the amazing bakers and bloggers who took the time to send in their delicious recipes and answer all of our questions thoughtfully and often with great humor: Elisabeth Prueitt and Chad Robertson (Tartine Bakery), Joanne Chang (Flour Bakery + Cafe), Josh Loeb and Zoe Nathan (Huckleberry Café & Bakery), Matt Lewis and Renato Poliafito (Baked), Michelle Gayer (Salty Tart), Olivia O'Neal (Sugar Mama's Bakeshop), Sandra Holl (Floriole Cafe & Bakery), Teresa Ulrich (Pearl Bakery), Angie Dudley (Bakerella), Aran Goyoaga (Cannelle et Vanille), Béatrice Peltre (La Tartine Gourmande), and Deb Perelman (Smitten Kitchen). To my co-workers and friends at Weldon Owen, LinkTV, and KQED who "endured" the endless onslaught of baked goods in exchange for honest feedback. To my friends and family who also gave great advice, especially my mom and brother who allowed me to use some of our "secret" family recipes. And to my patient and ever-loving husband who happily tasted nearly everything in the book, helped do the dishes, kept me sane, and supported me throughout this whole wonderful, crazy process.

From Eric Wolfinger: My heartfelt thanks to Emma Boys for allowing me to style and photograph the book in my own way. To Fontaine and Guiness McFadden for opening their family farmhouse where we truly baked "at home." To Julieann Moore, my talented co-baker, whose humor and hard work kept the kitchen going all day. To Chad and Liz, my mentors from Tartine, whose vision continues to inspire so many of us who baked there. To the friends who took me in while on the road. And to Kelly Puleio, my rockin' assistant whom I'm also lucky to call a friend.

Weldon Owen wishes to also thank the following people for their generous support in producing this book: Kimberly Chun, Judith Dunham, Rachel Lopez Metzger, Elizabeth Parson, and Tracy White Taylor.